melissa's®
DYPs™
THE PERFECT EVERYDAY POTATO COOKBOOK

Sharon Hernandez *and* Chef Ida Rodriguez

Published in the United States by World Variety Produce, Inc.

Library of Congress Control Number: 2014946862

ISBN-10: 0990644308
ISBN-13: 978-0-9906443-0-9
UPC: 045255-14744

Distributed by:
World Variety Produce, Inc.
PO Box 514599
Los Angeles, CA 90051

Photography:
Melissa's/World Variety
Produce, Inc.

To order, contact Melissa's:
800-588-0151
www.melissas.com
hotline@melissas.com

Printed in China
10 9 8 7 6 5 4 3 2 1

melissa's®
DYPs™
THE PERFECT EVERYDAY POTATO COOKBOOK

Sharon Hernandez *and* Chef Ida Rodriguez

Melissa's / World Variety Produce, Inc., is known for the freshest ideas in produce. Company founders Sharon and Joe Hernandez, along with their daughter, Melissa, have introduced exotic, conventional, and organic produce items to food lovers across the nation.

Melissa's / World Variety Produce, Inc., leads the industry in supplying delicious and delectable tasting fruits and vegetables to supermarkets and venues all over the world. In the professional culinary world, Melissa's has long been recognized as the extraordinary supplier for the freshest and tastiest fruits and vegetables. World-renowned chefs insist upon Melissa's Produce for their signature restaurants.

Melissa's consistently shares what's in season with you, to bring the flavors of the world to your kitchen. Please visit us at www.melissas.com and be sure to look and ask for Melissa's brand in your local produce department.

DUTCH YELLOW® POTATOES

Table *of* Contents

Introduction

Like so many other foods that are a staple in the American diet, the potato was first cultivated by those ancient foodies, the Aztecs, and then introduced to Europe by their Spanish conquerors. However, we can really thank Benjamin Franklin for popularizing the tuber to this country. It seems that old Ben, during his days as ambassador to France, had the good fortune to be invited to the dining table of King Louis XVI on the night of October 21, 1787, for a royal dinner that would prove to be pivotal in potato history.

The menu that night was prepared by Antoine Parmentier, a potato advocate trying to sell King Louis on this easy-to-grow crop as the answer to France's food security issues. The fare was an impressive twenty-course meal, with each dish featuring potatoes prepared in a different and tasty way. From soup to dessert, every course used potatoes as a base. The table was complemented by an array of biscuits, breads, and sauces also made with potato flour. Even the after-dinner coffee was laced with potato starch and that aforementioned dessert was a potato tart!

The potato did not really become popular in this county until Franklin returned to America singing the praises of the tuber from his experience at the Royal Court. Soon, because of Franklin's passionate efforts, the potato started to be farmed throughout the colonies. Cultivation of the crop spread quickly to remote regions of the western frontier because the potato produces very high yields with little tending on a small plot of land. Today the potato is the world's fourth largest food crop, behind rice, wheat, and corn.

Here in the U.S., the state of Idaho grows approximately 35% of the country's commercial potato crop. The success of this production is due to a perfect storm of environmental conditions. The volcanic characteristics of the region, which includes a part of the still very geologically active Yellowstone Park, have laid down eons of volcanic mineral residues known to be great soil enhancers for potato growing. Also, the state's cool but long sunny days during the spring and summer growing season very much mimic conditions found both in Ireland and the Peruvian Andes, the motherland of all potato varieties.

In the growing regions of Southern Idaho, add to these ideal soil and weather conditions an abundance of water from the many rivers winding through the countryside, fed by melting snows of the surrounding mountain ranges, creating the fertile Snake River Plain. It all makes this part of the planet one of the most productive potato growing regions in the world and the home of Melissa's Dutch Yellow® Potato.

Potatoes can be divided into two very broad categories based on texture, which depends upon the kind of starches they contain. Unfortunately, the two terms for a potato's texture comes with definition baggage that must be put aside, for a tuber is either "mealy" or "waxy"—in the good sense of these words! For instance, the familiar Idaho russet is a *mealy* potato, meaning that it cooks into a light, dry, and fluffy texture.

Dutch Yellow® Potatoes are considered *waxy* as they remain dense and moist when cooked. The DYP™ also cooks a lot quicker than other kinds of potatoes. It is also the only potato variety that is not light sensitive, so it does not turn a greenish hue when exposed to light for an extended length of time.

The naturally small and uniform size of the DYP™ is another characteristic that makes the variety a useful culinary tool. DYPs™ are a mellow shade of yellow inside and out, with a thin edible skin; they are packed with flavor and ready to bake, steam, boil, microwave, sauté, or grill whole.

The DYP™ is available twelve months of the year. The annual harvests of this tuber are from August through October. They're then cured in large, climate-controlled storage rooms until the crop is ready to sort, pack, and ship. Because of the variety's long-term storage characteristics, the harvest is packed on demand throughout the year as needed. The consistency of this year-round supply is what this cookbook celebrates.

Recipes are grouped according to the four seasons of the year. Because the DYP™ is available year-round, the home chef can use the revolving parade of seasonal fresh ingredients to enhance, support, and combine with the DYP™ throughout the harvest year. Its creamy texture and buttery flavor make the variety a versatile ingredient that pairs equally well with fish, fowl, or meat entrées.

Note: *When a recipe calls for cooked DYPs™, the preparation is simple. Place the DYPs™ in a large saucepan, cover with cold water, and bring to a boil. Cook until fork tender, about 6 to 10 minutes. Drain well, and proceed as directed.*

The **SPRING** recipe group consists of an array of fresh salad ideas that marry the DYP™ with the first leafy greens of the harvest season as well as other early spring crops. There are also several small plate appetizers, many tasty side dishes, some delicious light luncheon entrées, even a potato bread and potato cheesecake recipe!

The **SUMMER** grouping celebrates the grilling season with enough versions of potato salad to fill several picnic tables. For an interesting twist, try Gado Gado, a surprising pairing of peanut butter and DYPs™ that works scrumptiously. Of course, the grill itself is utilized to create delicious sides for the family backyard barbecue season. There is a tasty DYP™ pizza slathered in BBQ sauce and the wholly original PoTaco must be tasted to appreciate the unique flavor that comes from combining DYPs™, mushrooms, peppers, hot sauce, and yogurt in one wrap.

A hearty fare is the theme of the **FALL** section of DYP™ recipes. Lots of warming soups, creamy mashed dishes and some creative purées. The oven is the main implement used to create casseroles, pot pies and an assortment of baked comfort food side dishes. It's a time of seasonal transition, so these recipes go with cooler temperatures and falling leaves perfectly.

WINTER is a time of slow-cooked stews, gratins, and roasting recipes—this section contains many in each category. There are creamy chowders as well as a few very fortifying soups. A good breakfast meal is a sure-fire way to combat the season's blustery weather patterns, so there are several tasty dishes to start the day. In fact, this segment of the cookbook will guard against the winter like a heavy coat! Nor have we forgotten the need for a comforting after dinner treat around a roaring fireplace; the Chocolate DYP™ Cake or DYP™ Coconut Fudge recipes are guaranteed to warm toes with delicious decadence!

The U.S. consumer eats approximately 126 pounds of potatoes each year. We at Melissa's feel this book of 150 everyday recipes will no doubt help to increase that average as it introduces the home gourmet to new ways of enjoying DYPs™ twelve months a year.

Happy Cooking!
Sharon Hernandez *and* Melissa's Corporate Chef Ida Rodriguez

SPRING

DYP™ Salad *with* Dijon Vinaigrette

~~~~~~~~~~~~~~~ *makes 10 to 12 servings* ~~~~~~~~~~~~~~~

8 ounces French green beans, trimmed and cut into ½-inch pieces

3 pounds DYPs™, cut in half

2 tablespoons dry vermouth

2 tablespoons white wine vinegar

1 large shallot, chopped

1 tablespoon whole grain mustard

½ teaspoon salt, plus more to taste

Freshly ground black pepper to taste

⅔ cup extra virgin olive oil

2 tablespoons chopped parsley

Prepare an ice bath. Cook the green beans in a large saucepan of boiling salted water until crisp-tender, about 2 minutes. Drain. Transfer the green beans to the ice bath to stop the cooking, and then drain.

Cook the DYPs™ in a large pot of boiling salted water until just tender, about 12 minutes. (You don't want them falling apart.) Drain and then sprinkle the vermouth over the hot DYPs™. Toss gently and let stand 5 minutes. In a small bowl, whisk together the vinegar, shallots, mustard, salt, and pepper in a small bowl. Add the oil in a steady stream, whisking continuously. Pour the vinaigrette over the DYPs™ and toss gently to coat. Cool completely, and then toss in the green beans and parsley. Taste and season with additional salt and pepper if needed.

Composed Salad Platter

makes 4 servings

1 pound DYPs™

Sea salt and freshly ground black pepper to taste

2 pounds mixed salad greens, washed and dried

1 package Melissa's Peeled Baby Red Beets, quartered

1 pint cherry tomatoes, halved

1 yellow bell pepper, julienned

1 bunch green onions, sliced into rounds

4 hard-boiled eggs, halved

1 (5.1-ounce) can good-quality tuna, drained

Blue cheese or Italian salad dressing

Place the DYPs™ in a saucepan and cover with water. Set over high heat and bring to a gentle boil. Cook 5 to 8 minutes, or just until fork tender; drain. When cool enough to handle, gently flatten each DYP™ to about half its thickness with your hand, a kitchen mallet, or the bottom of a pan.

Set a grill pan over medium-high heat. Once hot, place the DYPs™ in the grill pan and cook for 2 to 3 minutes on each side, or until nice grill marks form. Remove from the pan and season with salt and pepper.

To assemble the salad, place the greens on a large platter. Arrange the rest of the components in rows over the greens. Serve with dressing on the side.

Springy DYP™ Salad

makes 6 to 8 servings

2 pounds DYPs™, cut in quarters

2 stalks celery, diced

2 cucumbers, diced

5 green onions, diced

1 red bell pepper, diced

½ cup mayonnaise, or to taste

Salt and freshly ground black pepper

Juice from ½ lemon

2 sprigs organic parsley, finely minced

In a large saucepan, cover the DYPs™ with cold water and bring to a boil. Cook until fork tender, about 6 to 10 minutes. Drain well, transfer to a mixing bowl, and let cool to room temperature.

Add the celery, cucumber, green onion, and pepper to the DYPs™; stir gently to combine. Fold in the mayonnaise to your taste and season with salt and pepper. Sprinkle with the lemon juice and parsley, and mix well to combine the ingredients. Cover and chill completely.

Creamy Chipotle Salad

makes 6 to 8 servings

2 pounds DYPs™

¼ cup fresh lime juice, divided

½ cup mayonnaise

2 chipotle chiles in adobo, minced

1 teaspoon adobo sauce

4 green onions, thinly sliced

2 tablespoons cilantro, chopped

Place the DYPs™ in a large saucepan. Cover with cold water and bring to a boil. Reduce the heat and cook for 8 to 12 minutes, or until the DYPs™ are fork tender. When just cool enough to handle, slice the DYPs™ into ½-inch slices and sprinkle with 2 tablespoons of the lime juice.

Let cool to room temperature, and then add the remaining ingredients. Toss gently until the DYPs™ are evenly coated.

Asian Bok Choy Salad

makes 6 to 8 servings

3 pounds DYPs™

12 ounces pearl onions

Olive oil for sautéing

Salt and freshly ground black pepper to taste

1 cup mayonnaise

1 teaspoon sugar

1 tablespoon soy sauce

1 teaspoon sesame oil

3 baby bok choy, trimmed and roughly chopped

1 green onion

¼ cup chopped cilantro

Salt to taste

Place the DYPs™ in a large saucepan and cover with cold, salted water. Bring to a boil and cook until fork tender, about 9 to 13 minutes. Drain and let cool.

While the DYPs™ are cooking, prepare an ice bath. Bring a small saucepan of water to a boil, and boil the pearl onions until tender, about 8 to 10 minutes. Drain and then immediately submerge the onions in the ice bath to cool. Peel the onions once they've cooled, and then season them with salt and pepper.

Set a medium pan over medium heat and add 1 to 2 teaspoons olive oil. Sauté the onions until they are translucent. Let cool, and then cut them in half.

In a small bowl, whisk together the mayonnaise, sugar, soy sauce, and sesame oil to make the dressing.

In large bowl, combine the DYPs™, onions, bok choy, cilantro, and dressing. Toss gently to combine. Serve warm or at room temperature.

Crabby DYP™ Salad *with* Sun-Dried Tomato Pesto Dressing

makes 4 to 6 servings

1½ pounds DYPs™, cut into quarters

Salt

1 cup Greek yogurt

1 jar Melissa's Sun-Dried Tomato Pesto

¼ cup Thousand Island dressing

Cayenne pepper to taste

6 stalks celery, thinly sliced

6 green onions, thinly sliced

1 pound lump crab meat, picked over

In a large saucepan, cover the DYPs™ with cold, salted water and bring to a boil over high heat. Reduce the heat and simmer 4 to 7 minutes, or until fork tender; drain and let cool.

In a large bowl, combine the yogurt, pesto, Thousand Island dressing, and cayenne. Add the celery, onions, crab meat, and DYPs™. Toss gently to combine. Serve immediately.

DYP™ Bites

makes 30 to 40 appetizer portions

1½ pound DYPs™

1 tablespoon olive oil

1 teaspoon kosher salt

DYP™ Filling:

¼ cup mayonnaise

2 tablespoons sweet pickle relish

1 teaspoon cider vinegar

1 teaspoon spicy brown mustard

¼ teaspoon freshly ground black pepper

¼ teaspoon salt

⅛ teaspoon hot sauce

⅛ teaspoon ground celery seed

½ teaspoon paprika

Fresh dill for garnish

Preheat the oven to 325° F. Toss the DYPs™, olive oil, and the kosher salt in a small bowl. Spread on a baking sheet and bake for 13 to 15 minutes, or until tender. Remove from the oven and let cool.

When cool enough to handle, cut each DYP™ in half lengthwise. Carefully scoop out the DYP™ pulp into a bowl, leaving the skin intact. Return the skins to the baking sheet and bake 10 more minutes, or until crisp. Let cool completely.

While the skins are baking, make the filling. Add the filling ingredients to the DYP™ pulp in the bowl. Mix and mash until well combined and quite smooth. Fill each DYP™ skin with the filling. Serve at room temperature or return to the oven for 5 to 8 minutes, or until warmed through. Sprinkle with paprika and garnish with fresh dill and more black pepper.

DYP™ *and* Veggie Salad

makes 6 to 8 servings

2 pounds DYPs™, cut in half

2 tablespoons apple cider vinegar

1 tablespoon olive oil

½ cup buttermilk

¼ cup Greek yogurt

¼ cup mayonnaise

1 tablespoon Dijon mustard

1 red bell pepper, julienned

½ cup chopped cucumber

½ cup sliced radishes

1 cup steamed sugar snap peas

¼ cup finely chopped fresh parsley

1 tablespoon grated lemon zest

1 garlic clove, minced

Salt and freshly ground black pepper to taste

In a medium saucepan, cover the DYPs™ with cold, salted water and bring to a boil. Cook for 7 to 11 minutes, or until fork tender. Drain and place in a large bowl. Sprinkle with the vinegar and oil and toss gently. Let cool completely.

When the DYPs™ have cooled, whisk together the buttermilk, yogurt, mayonnaise, and mustard in a large bowl. Stir in the bell pepper, cucumber, radishes, snap peas, parsley, lemon zest, and garlic. Season with salt and pepper to taste. Pour the buttermilk mixture over the DYP™ mixture, and then toss gently to coat. Cover and chill at least 1 hour and up to 24 hours before serving.

DYP™ Salad Trifle

makes 6 to 8 servings

Dressing:

1 cup mayonnaise

3 tablespoons sweet pickle juice

2 tablespoons yellow mustard

¼ teaspoon garlic salt

¼ teaspoon freshly ground black pepper

Salad:

1½ pounds DYPs™

3 stalks celery, thinly sliced

12 green olives, sliced

½ red onion, thinly sliced

1 cup sweet pickle slices

4 hard-boiled eggs, sliced

6 slices bacon, cooked and crumbled

Stir the dressing ingredients together in a small bowl and set aside.

In a large saucepan, cover the DYPs™ with cold water and bring to a boil over high heat. Reduce the heat and simmer 6 to 9 minutes, or until fork tender; drain. When cool, slice into ¼-inch-thick slices.

In a trifle dish, place the DYP™ slices evenly on the bottom. Drizzle with a little of the dressing. Next add the celery and green olives. Drizzle with a little more dressing. Add a layer of red onion, and then pickle slices. Drizzle with more dressing. Add a layer of egg and then top with the bacon. Drizzle with remaining dressing and serve.

Steak *and* DYP™ Salad

makes 6 to 8 servings

1½ pounds DYPs™, cut in half

2 tablespoons olive oil

1½ pounds flank steak

½ teaspoon salt

1 teaspoon freshly ground black pepper

1 pound asparagus, ends trimmed

1 red bell pepper, trimmed, seeded, and cut into fourths

1 red onion, peeled and cut into 8 wedges

Dressing:

½ cup red wine vinegar

⅓ cup olive oil

1 tablespoon coarse-grained mustard

1 teaspoon grated lemon zest

3 tablespoons fresh lemon juice

1 garlic clove, pressed

1 teaspoon salt

4 ounces blue cheese, crumbled

Preheat a grill to medium-high heat. Place the DYPs™ in a single layer in the center of a large piece of heavy-duty aluminum foil and drizzle with the olive oil. Bring up sides of the foil over the DYPs™, and double-fold the top and side edges to seal, making a packet. Season the steak with the salt and pepper.

Grill the DYPs™ (in their foil packet) and the steak for 7 to 8 minutes on each side. In the last 5 minutes of grilling, add the asparagus, bell pepper, and onions and grill for 4 to 5 minutes, or until tender. Remove the steak and vegetables from the grill and let stand for 10 minutes. Empty the DYPs™ into a large bowl.

While the meat is cooking, whisk together the dressing ingredients in a small bowl. Add half the dressing to the DYPs™ and mix gently.

Cut the steak diagonally across the grain into thin strips. Cut the asparagus into thirds and the bell pepper pieces into strips. Separate the onion layers. Toss together the steak, DYPs™, and grilled vegetables. Sprinkle with the blue cheese and drizzle with the remaining dressing.

DYP™ Stack Salad

1½ pounds DYPs™, diced

6 tablespoons extra virgin olive oil, divided

2 Roma tomatoes, sliced

4 mini cucumbers, diced

1 head baby frisée, shredded

½ cup crumbled blue cheese

2 tablespoons seasoned rice vinegar

Salt and freshly ground black pepper

Preheat the oven to 425° F.

Toss the DYPs™ with 2 tablespoons of the olive oil, and then place them on a baking sheet in a single layer. Roast in the oven until tender, about 10 to 13 minutes. Remove from the oven and let cool.

To make the stacks, start with a ring mold or large biscuit cutter in the center of each salad plate. Place a 1-inch-thick layer of DYPs™ in the bottom. Next add a tomato slice, and top that with diced cucumbers. Carefully remove the ring mold. Top with some frisée and blue cheese.

In a small bowl, combine the remaining 2 tablespoons oil with the vinegar, salt, and pepper. Drizzle over the salad and serve.

DYP™ Cucumber *and* Dill Salad

~~~~~~~~~~~~~~~~~~~~~ *makes 8 servings* ~~~~~~~~~~~~~~~~~~~~

1½ pounds DYPs™, cut in half

2 ears sweet corn, husks and silks removed

6 mini cucumbers

1 pint baby heirloom tomatoes, cut in half

1 teaspoon seasoned rice vinegar

½ cup Greek yogurt

¼ cup sour cream

2 tablespoons chopped fresh dill

Salt and freshly ground black pepper

Place the DYPs™ in a medium saucepan and cover with 2 inches of cold water. Bring to a boil over medium heat and cook 5 to 8 minutes, or until fork tender. Drain and let cool.

Grill the corn on a hot grill or a hot grill pan until warmed through and slightly charred. When cool enough to handle, slice the corn kernels from the ears with a knife. Quarter the cucumbers lengthwise and then cut them into bite-sized pieces. Place all of the veggies in a bowl and gently mix until combined. In another bowl, mix together the vinegar and the rest of the ingredients. Spoon the vinegar mixture over the veggies and toss gently to combine. Refrigerate for 30 minutes before serving.

DYP™ Salad Parfaits

makes 4 parfaits

½ cup green peas, cooked
(canned is fine)

½ cup diced celery

2 tablespoons capers

1 tablespoon minced fresh dill

¾ cup mayonnaise

1 tablespoon Dijon mustard

2 tablespoons fresh lemon juice

2 cups DYPs™, cooked, peeled, and sliced ½-inch thick (about 8 ounces uncooked)

½ red onion, thinly sliced

4 hard-boiled eggs, sliced ¼-inch thick

½ cup sliced dill pickles

Coarse sea salt and freshly ground black pepper

3-inch-long celery tops, for garnish

In a small bowl, gently mix the peas, diced celery, capers, dill, mayonnaise, mustard, and lemon juice together. Season to taste with salt and pepper.

Layer the DYPs™, red onion, eggs, pickles, and the pea mixture in 4 short drinking glasses or glass compotes. Repeat the layers, ending with the pea mixture on top. Garnish with celery sticks.

Mini Reuben Sandwiches

makes 16 appetizer servings

½ pound DYPs™, cut in half

2 tablespoons extra virgin olive oil

Salt and freshly ground black pepper to taste

8 slices rye bread

4 slices cooked corned beef

4 slices Swiss cheese

Melissa's Cream Style Horseradish

Thousand Island dressing

Preheat the oven to 425° F.

In a large bowl, combine the DYPs™, olive oil, salt, and pepper, and toss to coat. Spread them evenly on a baking sheet and roast until fork tender, about 8 to 11 minutes.

On another baking sheet, place half of the bread slices in a single layer. Top the bread with the corned beef and then the cheese. When the DYPs™ are done, increase the heat to broil and melt the cheese under the broiler. Remove from the broiler and begin building the sandwiches: Spread a thin layer of horseradish on the cheese, and then spread Thousand Island dressing on the rest of the bread. Top each sandwich and cut diagonally into fourths. Place a roasted DYP™ half on each sandwich quarter, secure with a toothpick, and serve.

Corned Beef *and* Cabbage Bites

makes 10 servings

½ pound DYPs™, cut in half

2 tablespoons extra virgin olive oil

Salt and freshly ground black pepper to taste

¼ cabbage, cut into 2-inch-square pieces

Thousand Island dressing

8 slices Swiss cheese, cut into small triangles

8 slices cooked corned beef, cut into small triangles

1 (16-ounce) jar sauerkraut

Preheat the oven to 425° F.

Combine the DYPs™, olive oil, salt, and pepper in a bowl, and toss to coat. Spread the DYP™ halves in a single layer on a baking sheet. Roast them in the oven until fork tender, about 8-11 minutes. Remove from the oven and let cool.

When the DYPs™ are cool, toss the cabbage pieces with enough Thousand Island dressing to lightly coat. To assemble the cabbage bites, top each piece of cabbage with a triangle of cheese and then 3 beef triangles. Top the beef with a bit of sauerkraut, finish with a roasted DYP™ half, and secure with a toothpick.

DYP™ *and* Caramelized Onion Pierogis

makes 6 to 8 servings

Filling:

2 cups cooked and mashed DYPs™

⅓ cup plain yogurt

⅓ cup crumbled blue cheese

2 tablespoons minced flat leaf parsley

½ teaspoon kosher salt

¼ teaspoon freshly ground black pepper

Dough:

2 eggs, room temperature, beaten

½ teaspoon kosher salt

⅓ cup room temperature water

2 cups unbleached all-purpose flour

Topping:

5 cups thinly sliced yellow onion

3 tablespoons grapeseed oil

2 tablespoons unsalted butter

2 pinches light brown sugar

4 pinches kosher salt

Mix the filling ingredients together in a bowl until thoroughly combined.

To make the dough, whisk together the water, salt, and eggs in a large bowl. Add the flour and stir to combine. Using your hands, knead the dough for about 3 to 5 minutes, or until well mixed and firm. Cover the bowl with plastic wrap and set aside for 30 minutes.

Lightly flour a flat surface and roll the dough out to ⅛-inch thick. Using a 3-inch biscuit cutter or a glass, cut as many rounds as possible from the dough. Re-roll the scraps and cut into more rounds.

Place about 1½ teaspoons of filling into the center of each dough round, filling all of the rounds before sealing. Using clean, dry hands, gently stretch and fold each round to create a half-moon shape, being careful to keep the filling inside and away from the edges. Press the edges together, using a little water to seal if necessary, and crimp the edges with a fork.

Heat the oil and butter in a large nonstick skillet over medium heat. Add the onions and 2 pinches of salt and sauté until the onions are translucent. Add 1 pinch of brown sugar and continue to sauté until the onions begin to brown. Add another pinch of brown sugar and the remaining salt and stir to combine. Reduce the heat to low.

Heat a large pot of water to a boil. Reduce the heat to medium and carefully place 6 pierogis at a time into the water. Gently stir to ensure the pierogis don't stick to the bottom of the pot. In about 3 minutes, the pierogis will rise to the surface. Continue to cook another 3 minutes after they float to the top.

Increase the heat under the caramelized onions. Remove the pierogis from the boiling water with a slotted spoon, and place them in the pan with the onions. Toss to coat, and continue cooking and adding additional pierogis until they are all browned.

Sweet Pot Stickers *with* Ginger-Lemon Sauce

makes 26 to 28 pot stickers

1 pound DYPs™

2 tablespoons honey

1 pinch kosher salt

26 to 28 pot sticker wrappers

Vegetable oil, for browning

Ginger-Lemon Sauce:

½ cup Greek yogurt

1 teaspoon minced fresh ginger

1 teaspoon granulated sugar

Zest and juice of 1 lemon

In a large saucepan, cover the DYPs™ with cold water and bring to a boil over high heat. Reduce the heat and simmer for 5 to 8 minutes, or until fork tender; drain. Using a potato ricer, press the DYPs™ into a medium bowl. Stir in the honey and salt. Lay a single pot sticker wrapper on a flat surface. Moisten the edge of the wrapper with water. Place a small spoonful of the DYP™ mixture in the middle of the wrapper and fold the wrapper over to form a half-circle. Crimp the edges with a fork to seal. Repeat with the remaining wrappers.

Fill a medium stockpot halfway with water and bring to a gentle boil. Carefully drop the pot stickers into the boiling water, one by one, without over-crowding the pot. Cook until the pot stickers are translucent, 2 to 4 minutes. Drain on parchment paper.

Place the oil in a nonstick skillet and set over medium heat. When hot, add the pot stickers to brown them, about 30 seconds on both sides. Drain on a paper towel.

Whisk the sauce ingredients together in a small bowl until smooth.

To serve, place the pot stickers on a platter or individual appetizer plates and drizzle with the sauce.

George's DYP™ Sushi Rolls

makes 4 rolls (24 pieces)

1½ cups sushi rice

1¾ cups water

½ cup seasoned rice vinegar

1 tablespoon canola oil

¼ cup granulated sugar

1 teaspoon kosher salt

3 tablespoons mayonnaise

½ teaspoon hot sauce
(such as Tabasco®)

4 sheets nori (seaweed) paper

½ pound DYPs™, boiled and pressed
through a potato ricer

8 asparagus spears, cooked

4 Melissa's Pimientos Del
Piquillo Peppers

Salt to taste

Black sesame seeds for seasoning

Rinse the rice in a strainer until the water runs clear. In a medium saucepan, add the rice and the water. Bring to a boil, reduce the heat, cover, and simmer for 20 minutes. Remove from the heat and set aside until the rice is cool enough to handle.

In a small saucepan, combine the vinegar, oil, sugar, and salt. Cook over medium heat until the sugar dissolves. Let cool, and then stir into the cooked rice.

In a small bowl, mix together the mayonnaise and hot sauce. Place a nori sheet on a sushi mat, shiny-side down. Spread a layer of rice over the nori. Using your hands, press a layer of DYPs™ over the rice. Add 2 asparagus spears and 1 piquillo pepper along the center. Season with salt and sprinkle with the sesame seeds. Spoon a bit of the mayonnaise mixture over the peppers. Placing your thumbs on back of sushi mat, begin rolling away from you, supporting the filling with your fingers. Roll until edge of the nori is under the sushi roll. Shape the roll by pressing lightly with both hands. Remove the sushi mat and slice the roll into 6 pieces. Repeat for the remaining rolls.

DYP™ Croquettes

makes 40 croquettes

2 pounds DYPs™

2 tablespoons milk

Salt

½ teaspoon freshly ground black pepper

8 ounces mozzarella, shredded

¼ cup grated Parmesan

1 tablespoon minced green onion

3 tablespoons all-purpose flour

5 eggs, divided

2½ cups panko breadcrumbs

Neutral oil for frying

In a large saucepan, cover the DYPs™ with cold, salted water and bring to a boil over high heat. Lower the heat to a simmer and cook until the DYPs™ are fork tender, about 8 to 12 minutes. Drain the DYPs™ and let cool completely.

Press the DYPs™ through a potato ricer into a large bowl. Stir in the milk, and then season with salt and pepper to taste. Add the cheeses, green onion, and flour. Stir in 1 egg. Mix thoroughly and form into 20 balls. Divide each ball into 2 oblong shapes.

Line a baking sheet with parchment paper. Lightly beat the remaining 4 eggs in a shallow bowl and place the breadcrumbs in another shallow bowl. Dip each croquette into the egg, letting the excess drip off, and then roll in breadcrumbs to coat. Transfer to the lined baking sheet and repeat with the remaining croquettes.

Pour enough oil to come ½-inch up the sides of a heavy 12-inch skillet set over medium to medium-high heat. Test the oil with a pinch of breadcrumbs. When the crumbs sizzle, the oil is ready. Fry the croquettes in batches, turning occasionally until golden brown, about 4 to 5 minutes per batch. Transfer to paper towels to drain and serve immediately with a béchamel sauce or garlic aïoli.

Note: *A potato ricer resembles an oversized garlic press. It has two long handles, one with a perforated basket at the end, the other with a flat surface that fits into the basket. The DYPs™ are placed in the basket, and then the flat surface is pushed down into the basket by pressing the handles together, forcing the potato through the holes and creating the fluffiest mashed potatoes ever.*

DYP™ Frittata

makes 6 to 8 servings

1 tablespoon extra virgin olive oil

1 tablespoon unsalted butter

12 ounces DYPs™, diced

Salt and freshly ground black pepper to taste

12 eggs

1 teaspoon dried oregano

1 teaspoon dried thyme

1 pint Melissa's Baby Heirloom Tomatoes, cut in half

1 cup Melissa's fresh basil chiffonade

8 ounces cream cheese, cubed

Preheat the oven to 425° F.

In a large, ovensafe sauté pan, heat the olive oil and butter over medium heat. Add the DYPs™, season with salt and pepper, and sauté about 7 minutes, or until fork tender. In a large bowl, whisk together the eggs, oregano, and thyme. Add the mixture to the sauté pan and sprinkle evenly with the tomatoes, basil, and cream cheese. Place the sauté pan in the oven and bake for 20 to 25 minutes, or until set. Remove from the oven and cut into wedges to serve.

Scarborough Fair Frittata

makes 6 to 8 servings

2 cups cooked and mashed DYPs™ (about 1 pound fresh)

6 eggs

3 tablespoons minced flat leaf parsley

½ teaspoon minced fresh sage

½ teaspoon minced fresh rosemary

½ teaspoon minced fresh thyme

2 teaspoons sea salt

1 teaspoon freshly ground black pepper

3 tablespoons olive oil

Place the cooked and mashed DYPs™ in a medium mixing bowl. Add the eggs and whisk together until smooth. Add the fresh herbs, salt, and pepper, and then whisk to combine.

Preheat the broiler. Heat the oil in a large, ovenproof sauté pan over medium-high heat. Test the oil with a bit of DYP™ mixture. If it sizzles, the oil is ready. Carefully pour the mixture into the pan and cook for about 6 to 7 minutes until the frittata is two-thirds set. Lower the heat to medium, cover the pan, and continue cooking another 5 to 6 minutes, or until the frittata is completely set.

Uncover the pan and place it under the broiler for 3 minutes, or until the top of the frittata is nicely browned.

Veggie Hash *and* Eggs

makes 4 servings

2 tablespoons vegetable oil

½ cup diced yellow onion

1 package Melissa's Peeled and
Steamed Red Beets, diced

½ pound DYPs™, diced

2 tablespoons Melissa's Cream
Style Horseradish

2 tablespoons apple cider vinegar

2 cups beet greens, chopped

Kosher salt and freshly ground
black pepper

4 large eggs

4 slices pumpernickel bread,
toasted and buttered (optional)

Add the oil to a large sauté pan over medium heat. When the oil begins to
lightly sizzle, add the onion and beets. Sauté 5 minutes, until the onions are
translucent, and then add the DYPs™. Sprinkle with salt and pepper and sauté
another 10 to 12 minutes.

In a small bowl, whisk together the creamed horseradish and apple cider
vinegar. Pour over the DYP™ mixture in the pan and stir to combine. Add the
beet greens and season to taste with salt and pepper. Cover the pan for
1 minute, or just until the greens begin to wilt. As soon as the
greens begin to wilt, break
1 egg into a small ramekin,
and then gently pour the
egg over the DYP™ mixture,
being careful not to break
the yolk. Repeat around
the pan with the remaining
eggs. Cover and cook 6 to 7
minutes, or until the eggs are
set to your liking. Serve over
toasted pumpernickel
if desired.

Vichyssoise

makes 6 servings

1½ cups diced DYPs™

1 package Melissa's Belgian Style Leeks or 2 leeks, well cleaned

2 tablespoons unsalted butter

2 cups vegetable or chicken broth

2 cups water, plus more for thinning

¾ teaspoon sea salt

White pepper to taste

Chives for garnish

Place diced DYPs™ in a bowl and cover with water to prevent discoloration. Slice the leeks in half lengthwise, then cut crosswise into 1-inch pieces.

Set a large stock pot over low heat and add the butter. Add the leeks and cook, stirring occasionally, until softened. Drain the DYPs™ and add them to the leeks along with 2 cups fresh water, the vegetable or chicken broth, and sea salt. Increase the heat to high and bring to a boil, and then reduce the heat to a simmer. Cook, covered, for 30 minutes, or until the DYPs™ are very soft. Use an immersion blender or place the soup in a blender, in batches if needed, and purée until smooth. (Be careful with hot liquids and blenders!) Return the puréed soup to the pan and add water to reach the desired consistency. Let the soup chill to room temperature, and then cover and store in the refrigerator until cold. Before serving, taste for seasoning and adjust as needed. Garnish with fresh chives.

DYP™ Beef Pie

makes 6 to 8 servings

Cooking spray

1½ pounds ground beef

2 cups breadcrumbs

1 tablespoon Italian seasoning

2 cups chopped onions, divided

2 large eggs, lightly beaten

1 teaspoon salt

1 teaspoon freshly ground black pepper

2 tablespoons olive oil

4 cups shredded DYPs™

8 ounces shredded Mexican four-cheese blend

1 tomato, chopped, for garnish

Preheat the oven to 375° F.

Spray the bottom and sides of a 9-inch springform pan with cooking spray.

Combine the ground beef, breadcrumbs, Italian seasoning, 1 cup of the chopped onions, eggs, salt, and pepper in a large bowl. Press the beef mixture into the bottom and up the sides of the springform pan; it will be approximately ⅜-inch thick. Bake for 10 to 15 minutes.

While the beef is baking, heat the olive oil in a large skillet over medium-high heat. Add the remaining cup of onion and the shredded DYPs™. Sauté for 10 minutes, stirring occasionally to prevent sticking.

Remove the beef mixture from oven, fill with the sautéed onion and DYP™ mixture, and sprinkle evenly with the cheese. Increase the heat to 375°F and return the pie to the oven for 20 to 25 minutes, or until the top is lightly browned. Garnish the finished pie with the chopped tomato.

DYP™–Stuffed Chicken Thighs

makes 8 servings

8 boneless, skinless chicken thighs

8 ounces DYPs™, shredded

16 spears fresh asparagus, ends trimmed

6 ounces Swiss cheese, sliced into strips

1 Portobello mushroom, gills and stem removed, sliced into strips

Kosher salt and freshly ground black pepper to taste

3 tablespoons extra virgin olive oil

2 cups chicken broth

Preheat the oven to 375° F.

With a kitchen mallet, pound the chicken thighs to half of their thickness. Top each thigh evenly with some of the shredded DYPs™, asparagus, cheese, and mushrooms. Roll the chicken up around the stuffing and secure with toothpicks.

In a large, ovenproof skillet, heat the olive oil over high heat. Add the chicken and sear on all sides. Add the chicken broth and stir, scraping the bottom of the pan to release any cooked bits of chicken. Place the pan in the oven and bake for about 25 minutes, or until an instant-read thermometer inserted into the center of the chicken rolls reads at least 165° F.

Salmon *with* Lemon-Herb Sauce and Scalloped DYPs™

1 (2-pound) fresh salmon fillet

4 DYPs™, sliced very thinly

Kosher salt and freshly ground black pepper to taste

½ teaspoon dried dill

1 tablespoon extra virgin olive oil

1 tablespoon unsalted butter

Lemon-Herb Sauce:

2 tablespoons minced shallot

¼ cup white wine

Juice of ½ lemon

6 tablespoons (3 ounces) unsalted butter

1 tablespoon minced fresh dill

1 tablespoon minced fresh chives

1 pinch freshly ground black pepper

1 pinch cayenne pepper

Preheat the oven to 350° F.

Lay the salmon, flesh-side up, on a work surface. Layer the DYP™ slices in rows slightly overlapping each other on the top of the salmon. Make one layer to completely cover the top and season with the salt, pepper, and dried dill.

Set a large oven-safe skillet over medium-high heat and add the olive oil and butter. Carefully transfer the fish to the skillet, skin-side down and DYP™-side up, and sear the fish for 2 minutes. Place the skillet in the oven and bake for 8 to 10 minutes. Remove from the oven, tent with foil, and set aside.

While the salmon is cooking, make the sauce. Combine the shallot, wine, and lemon juice in a small saucepan and bring to a boil over medium-high heat. Reduce the heat and simmer until the mixture is reduced, about 5 to 7 minutes. Stir in the butter one tablespoon at a time, and then add the herbs and seasonings.

To serve, place the fish on a platter and top with the sauce.

Fish *and* Chips

1 pound DYPs™, thinly sliced

Canola oil for frying

Smoked paprika to taste

Salt and freshly ground black pepper to taste

1 pound fresh cod fillets

1 (12-ounce) bottled beer

2 cups all-purpose flour

In a high-sided pan, add enough canola oil to come 1 inch up the sides and set over medium-high heat. When the oil is hot—about 360 to 375°F, but not smoking—fry the DYPs™ until golden brown. Drain on paper towels and season immediately with the paprika, salt, and pepper.

Pour the beer into a medium mixing bowl. Sift 1½ cups of the flour into the beer, whisking gently until just combined. Place the remaining ½ cup of flour in a shallow bowl. Pat the fish dry and season both sides with paprika, salt, and pepper. Coat the fish in the beer batter, shaking off any excess, and then dredge in the flour. Slide the fillets into the hot oil. Fry the fish, turning frequently, until deep golden and cooked through, about 4 to 5 minutes. Drain on paper towels and serve immediately with the DYPs™.

Greek DYPs™

1 tablespoon unsalted butter

1 tablespoon canola oil

1½ pounds DYPs™, cut in half

2 tablespoons oregano leaves, minced

1 tablespoon organic lemon zest

2 tablespoons fresh lemon juice

1 tablespoon minced garlic

1 teaspoon sea salt

Freshly ground black pepper to taste

Heat the oil and butter in a large skillet over medium heat. Add the DYP™ halves in a single layer. Cook until browned, about 5 minutes. Turn the halves over, being careful not to break them, and brown the other side. Reduce the heat to low, cover, and cook 3 to 5 minutes, or until tender throughout.

While the DYPs™ are cooking, mix the remaining ingredients in small bowl. When the DYPs™ are tender, add the lemon-garlic mixture and stir gently to coat. Cook until the mixture is fragrant and warm.

Herbed DYPs™

makes 4 to 6 servings

1½ pounds DYPs™, cut in half

6 sprigs thyme, de-stemmed

6 sprigs rosemary, de-stemmed

2 to 3 tablespoons extra virgin olive oil

Salt and freshly ground black pepper to taste

Preheat the oven to 425° F.

Toss the DYPs™, herbs, and olive oil together in a large bowl. Spread the coated DYPs™ evenly in a sheet pan and season with salt and pepper. Roast in the oven for 11 to 14 minutes, or until golden brown and fork tender.

Roasted DYPs™ *with* Jalapeño Vinaigrette

~~~~~ *makes 6 to 8 servings* ~~~~~

3 pounds DYPs™, quartered

¼ cup olive oil, or as needed to coat

Salt

3 jalapeño chiles, seeded and deveined

2 cups chopped cilantro

1½ shallots, chopped

2 cloves garlic, chopped

¼ cup extra virgin olive oil

3 tablespoons cider vinegar

½ teaspoon salt

Freshly ground black pepper

½ cup cotija cheese

Preheat the oven to 425° F. Place the DYPs™ on a sheet pan, drizzle with ¼ cup olive oil (or as needed to coat), and sprinkle with the salt. Toss to coat evenly. Place in the oven and roast for 12 to 17 minutes, or until fork tender. Remove and let cool.

While the DYPs™ are roasting, coarsely chop the jalapeños and pulse in a food processor. Add the cilantro, shallots, garlic, oil, and vinegar, and pulse until finely chopped. Gently toss with the cooled DYPs™. Taste and season with additional salt and pepper if needed. Top with cotija cheese.

Note: *The vinaigrette can be made 1 day ahead. Cover and chill until ready to use.*

DYPs™ Parmesano

makes 4 to 6 servings

2 pounds DYPs™, cut in quarters

2 tablespoons olive oil

1 teaspoon salt

Freshly ground black pepper

4 tablespoons (¼ cup) butter or margarine, melted

2 cloves garlic, minced

⅓ cup fresh lemon juice

⅔ cup Parmesan cheese

Preheat the oven to 425° F. Toss the DYPs™ with the oil, salt, and pepper. Spread on a baking sheet and roast for 11 to 16 minutes, or until tender.

While the DYPs™ are baking, combine the butter, garlic, and lemon juice in a small bowl. Pour over the cooked DYPs™, stirring gently to coat. Reduce the oven temperature to 350°F, cover, and bake the DYPs™ another 20 minutes. Uncover, sprinkle with Parmesan cheese, and bake 10 to 15 minutes, or until the cheese is melted and golden brown.

Raquel's Chile Lime DYPs™

makes 4 to 6 servings

2 pounds DYPs™

½ teaspoon salt

2 tablespoons fresh lime juice

½ teaspoon Hatch Chile powder
(such as Don Enrique)

In a large saucepan, cover the DYPs™ with cold water and bring to a boil over high heat. Reduce the heat and simmer 8 to 12 minutes, or until fork tender; drain. When cool enough to handle, cut into quarters and sprinkle with the salt. Sprinkle with the lime juice and chile powder, and mix well. Serve at room temperature.

Roasted DYP™
and Scallop Sauté

makes 4 to 6 servings

1½ pounds DYPs™, cut in half

4 tablespoons extra virgin olive oil, divided

Kosher salt and freshly ground black pepper to taste

1 green bell pepper, chopped

6 Melissa's Pimientos Del Piquillo Peppers, chopped

1 sweet onion, chopped

1 pound fresh scallops, side muscle removed

Juice of 1 lime

Preheat the oven to 425° F.

Toss the DYPs™ with 2 tablespoons of the olive oil and season with the salt and pepper. Place in a single layer on a baking sheet and roast in the oven for 10 minutes.

In a sauté pan, heat the other 2 tablespoons of olive oil over high heat. Add the bell pepper, piquillo peppers, onion, and scallops and sauté for 5 minutes, stirring often. Add the roasted DYPs™ and heat through. Turn off the heat and add the lime juice. Stir and serve hot over steamed rice.

Shallot *and* Garlic Mashed DYP™

~~~~~~~~~~~~~~~ *makes 6 to 8 servings* ~~~~~~~~~~~~~~~

2 pounds DYPs™, cut in half

3 tablespoons unsalted butter

5 shallots, finely minced

2 cloves garlic, finely minced

1 teaspoon salt

¼ teaspoon white pepper

½ teaspoon cider vinegar

1 cup milk

In a medium saucepan, cover the DYPs™ with cold water and bring to a boil. Cook for 7 to 11 minutes, or until fork tender. Drain and return to the pan.

Set another sauté pan over medium heat and add the butter. Sauté the shallots and garlic until soft, and then stir in the salt and pepper. Add the milk and cider vinegar, and heat gently without boiling. Add the hot milk mixture to the DYPs™, and mash with potato masher. Taste and adjust the seasoning as needed. Serve immediately.

Steve's Minty DYPs™

makes 4 to 6 servings

1½ pounds DYPs™, quartered

4 tablespoons olive oil, divided

Salt and pepper

1½ tablespoons flour

3 tablespoons mint jelly

Preheat the oven to 375° F.

Toss the DYPs™ with 2 tablespoons of the olive oil, and then place on a baking sheet in a single layer. Roast in the oven until tender, about 10 to 13 minutes. Cool slightly for 20 minutes, and then toss with the flour.

Heat a medium skillet over high heat. Add the remaining 2 tablespoons of olive oil and sauté the DYPs™ for 5 minutes, or until crispy. Remove the skillet from the heat and add the mint jelly, stirring until the jelly melts and coats the DYPs™.

Creamy Spinach

makes 6 to 8 servings

½ pound fresh spinach

2 pounds DYPs™, cut into quarters

Salt

¾ cup buttermilk, warmed

4 tablespoons (¼ cup) unsalted butter, melted

½ teaspoon freshly ground black pepper

Bring a medium saucepan of water to a boil. Add the spinach and cook 1 to 2 minutes, or just until wilted. Remove the spinach from the water with a large slotted spoon to drain.

In a large saucepan, cover the DYPs™ with cold, salted water and bring to a boil over high heat. Lower the heat to a simmer and cook until fork tender, about 6 to 10 minutes. Drain, return to the pan, and mash with a potato masher to the desired consistency. Stir in the warm buttermilk, melted butter, pepper, and spinach. Taste and adjust the seasoning with salt and pepper, if needed, and stir just until blended.

Colcannon

makes 4 servings

1 pound DYPs™, quartered

3 tablespoons olive oil, divided

1¾ cups Brussels sprouts, trimmed and thinly sliced

½ cup sliced green onion, plus more for garnish

1 clove garlic, minced

Sea salt and white pepper to taste

½ cup plain Greek yogurt

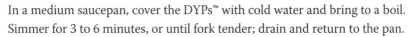

In a medium saucepan, cover the DYPs™ with cold water and bring to a boil. Simmer for 3 to 6 minutes, or until fork tender; drain and return to the pan.

Heat 2 tablespoons of the olive oil in a sauté pan over medium heat. Add the Brussels sprouts and sauté for 5 minutes. Sprinkle with sea salt and white pepper, and then add the green onions and garlic. Sauté 1 to 2 minutes, or just until the garlic is fragrant. Turn off the heat.

Add the remaining tablespoon olive oil and the Greek yogurt to the DYPs™ and mash with a potato masher. Fold in the Brussels sprouts mixture, season to taste with sea salt and white pepper, and garnish with the remaining green onion.

For leftovers, form the Colcannon into patties and pan fry in olive oil about 2 minutes per side, or until warmed through and golden brown. Serve with Greek yogurt and applesauce.

Dancing Cheesecake

makes 10 to 12 servings

Crust:

1 tablespoon unsalted butter, melted, divided

18 Oreo cookies, crushed

2 tablespoons granulated sugar

Pinch of kosher salt

Filling:

1 pound DYPs™, boiled

3 (8-ounce) packages cream cheese, at room temperature

1 cup granulated sugar

3 eggs

1 cup heavy cream

1 teaspoon scraped vanilla bean seeds

2 teaspoons ground nutmeg

Preheat the oven to 350° F.

For the crust, brush a 9-inch springform pan with some of the butter. Combine the crushed cookies with the remaining butter, the sugar, and salt in a medium bowl. Press the cookie mixture into the bottom of the springform pan. Bake for 15 minutes. Let cool.

Press the DYPs™ through a potato ricer into the bowl of a stand mixer. Add the cream cheese, and then beat the mixture until fluffy. With the mixer running, gradually add the sugar. Add the eggs, one at a time, mixing well after each addition. Add the cream, vanilla bean seeds, and nutmeg, and mix well. Pour the mixture into the springform pan. Bake for 45 minutes to 1 hour, or until the center is set. Remove from the oven and let cool at least 1 hour. Refrigerate until ready to serve.

DYP™ Date Bread

makes one 9 x 5-inch loaf

3 to 3½ cups all-purpose flour, divided

¼ cup sugar

1 packet rapid rise yeast

½ teaspoon salt

⅔ cup water

¼ cup safflower oil, plus more for oiling the baking pan

1 egg

⅓ cup cooked DYPs™ (about 6 ounces raw)

¾ cup chopped, pitted dates

In large bowl, combine 1 cup of the flour with the sugar, yeast, and salt. Combine the water and oil in a small saucepan over medium heat until very warm, about 125°F to 130°F. Gradually stir the warm liquids into the dry ingredients. Stir in the egg. Pass the cooked DYPs™ through a potato ricer to remove the skins, and then add the DYPs™ to the flour mixture. Add more flour as needed to make a soft dough. Turn the dough onto a lightly floured surface and knead until smooth, about 6 to 8 minutes. Cover and let rest on the floured surface 10 minutes.

Oil a 9 x 5-inch loaf pan. After the dough rests, knead the dates into the dough, dusting the surface with more flour if needed. Roll the dough into an 8 x 12-inch rectangle. Roll up tightly from the short side, as for a jelly roll. Pinch the seam and ends to seal. Place, seam-side down, in the loaf pan. Cover and let rise in a warm, draft-free place until doubled in size, about 35 to 45 minutes.

While the dough is rising, preheat the oven to 350°F. Bake the loaf for 35 minutes or until the crust turns golden. Turn out from the pan and cool on a wire rack.

DUTCH YELLOW® POTATOES

SUMMER

DYPs™ O'Brien

~~~~~~~~~~~~~~~ *makes 6 servings* ~~~~~~~~~~~~~~~

2 tablespoons butter

1 pound DYPs™, diced

⅓ cup diced green bell pepper

⅓ cup diced red bell pepper

⅓ cup diced yellow bell pepper

1 medium sweet onion, diced

2 cloves garlic, minced

½ teaspoon sea salt

½ teaspoon freshly ground black pepper

Heat the butter in large skillet over medium heat. Add the DYPs™, bell peppers, onion, garlic, salt, and pepper to the pan. Stir to combine and let cook 5 to 8 minutes, stirring occasionally, until the DYPs™ are tender.

DYP™ Southwest Hash

makes 4 to 6 servings

2 tablespoons olive oil

2 garlic cloves, minced

1 cup corn kernels

1 cup diced tomatoes

½ cup diced green onions, white and green parts

½ teaspoon ground cumin

1½ cup shiitake mushrooms, quartered

1½ pounds DYPs™, diced

½ cup chicken or vegetable broth

Salt and freshly ground black pepper to taste

Heat the oil in large sauté pan over medium heat. Add the garlic and cook for about 30 seconds, being careful not to burn the garlic. Add the remaining ingredients and season to taste with salt and pepper. Cover and cook about 5 minutes, or until the DYPs™ and mushrooms are tender. Uncover and continue cooking until all the liquid is absorbed.

Three Chile DYPs™

~~~~~~~~~~~~~~~~ *makes 4 to 6 servings* ~~~~~~~~~~~~~~~~

1 pound DYPs™, cut in half

4 ounces cipollini onions (about 4 onions), diced

¼ cup extra virgin olive oil

4 sprigs rosemary, de-stemmed

4 sprigs thyme, de-stemmed

Salt and freshly ground black pepper to taste

Garlic Chile Butter:

3 tablespoons unsalted butter, at room temperature

3 jalapeño chiles, seeded and minced

3 red Fresno chiles, minced

¼ teaspoon salt

3 cloves garlic, minced

Pinch of cayenne pepper

Preheat the oven to 425° F.

In a large bowl, gently toss the DYPs™, onions, olive oil, rosemary, and thyme until well coated. Place in a single layer on a baking pan and roast for 10 to 13 minutes, or until fork tender. Season with salt and black pepper to taste.

While the DYPs™ are cooking, combine all the ingredients for the garlic chile butter in a microwave-safe bowl. When the DYPs™ are done, melt the garlic chile butter in the microwave or on the stovetop and pour over the roasted DYPs™. Gently mix and serve immediately.

Three-Alarm
Roasted DYPs™

~~~~~~ *makes 8 servings* ~~~~~~

2 pounds DYPs™, cut in half

2 serrano chiles, sliced into rings

¼ cup extra virgin olive oil

1 teaspoon kosher salt

1 teaspoon freshly ground black pepper

Preheat the oven to 425° F.

In a mixing bowl, combine all the ingredients and spread onto a baking sheet. Roast for 15 to 20 minutes, or until the DYPs™ are fork tender and golden brown.

Grilled Fries

makes 6 servings

1½ pounds DYPs™

Salt and freshly ground
black pepper to taste

Ketchup, aïoli, malt vinegar,
or your favorite condiment

In a large saucepan, cover the DYPs™ with cold water and bring to a boil. Cook for 6 to 9 minutes, or until fork tender; drain. Gently smash each DYP™ to about half its thickness with your hands, a kitchen mallet, or the bottom of a pan.

Heat a grill pan over high heat. When hot, place the DYPs™ on the pan and cook until nice grill marks form, about 2 to 3 minutes per side. Remove from the pan, season with salt and pepper, and serve with your favorite condiments.

Summertime Stuffed DYPs™

Makes 18 to 20 appetizer size portions

3 pounds DYPs™

2 tablespoons unsalted butter

1 cup Greek yogurt

½ cup chopped chives

1 sprig rosemary, de-stemmed
and leaves chopped

3 sprigs thyme, de-stemmed

Salt and freshly ground
black pepper to taste

6 ounces cheddar cheese, grated

2 tablespoons finely chopped
Italian parsley

Chile powder (optional)

Preheat the oven to 425°F.

On a baking sheet, bake the DYPs™ for 16 to 20 minutes, or until they are
fork tender. Remove them from the oven and place on a cutting board. (Leave
the oven on.) When they are cool enough to handle, slice each DYP™ in half
lengthwise. With a small teaspoon, carefully scoop out the flesh from the skin.

In a large bowl, combine the flesh with the butter, yogurt, chives, rosemary,
and thyme. Stir together until the mixture is smooth. Season with salt and
pepper to taste.

Stuff each DYP™ skin with the DYP™ mixture. Top with the cheese and
return to the oven until the cheese is melted and bubbly. Sprinkle with the
parsley and, if desired, some chile powder for a spicier dish. Serve warm or
at room temperature.

Cheesy Tots

serves 4

Canola oil, for frying

1 pound DYPs™

1 Melissa's perfect sweet onion,
cut in half and thinly sliced

Salt

1 cup shredded cheddar cheese

In a deep fryer or high-sided pan, pour enough oil to come ½ inch up the side. Heat the oil to 360°F.

Carefully place the DYPs™ in the hot oil, being sure not to overcrowd the pan. Fry until golden brown, about 3 to 5 minutes, and drain on paper towels. When cool enough to handle, place the DYPs™ on a cutting board and slightly smash them with a metal spatula, one by one. Carefully place them back into the oil and fry them for another 2 to 3 minutes, or until they are crispy on the outside. Drain them on paper towels and season with salt.

Preheat the broiler.

In the same oil, fry the onion slices until crisp and golden or slightly dark brown. Drain them on paper towels.

Lightly coat a baking sheet with cooking spray. Place the fried DYPs™ on the sheet and sprinkle with the onions and the cheese. Place the DYPs™ under the broiler and cook until the cheese is melted and bubbly. Serve immediately.

DYP™ Gnocchi
with Maple Applesauce

~~~~~~~~~~~~~~~~ *makes 4 to 6 servings* ~~~~~~~~~~~~~~~~

1 pound DYPs™	1 pinch kosher salt
3 egg yolks	1 cup all-purpose flour
¼ teaspoon ground nutmeg	2 tablespoons unsalted butter
¼ teaspoon ground cinnamon	½ cup maple syrup
¼ teaspoon granulated sugar	2 Granny Smith apples, peeled, cored, and diced small

Preheat the oven to 425°F.

Arrange the DYPs™ on a baking sheet and bake for 20 minutes, or until slightly overcooked. When cool enough to handle, pass through a potato ricer.

Place the mashed DYPs™ on the counter in a mound with a well in the middle. Add the egg yolks, nutmeg, cinnamon, sugar and salt to the well. Mix the DYPs™ into the center of the well by hand, combining well. Sprinkle with ½ cup of flour and press the mixture down. Fold the dough over itself and press down again. Sprinkle on more flour, little by little, folding and pressing the dough until it just holds together. If the mixture is too dry, add another egg yolk or a little water. If it is too sticky, add a little flour. The dough should give under slight pressure. Keeping the work surface and the dough lightly floured, cut the dough into 4 pieces. Roll each piece into a rope about ½-inch in diameter. Cut each rope into ½-inch-long pieces. Take each piece and squish it lightly with a fork to form a gnocchi shape. As you shape the gnocchi, dust them lightly with flour and scatter them on baking sheets lined with parchment paper.

Bring a large pot of salted water to a boil. Drop in the gnocchi. When they rise to the surface, cook for about 90 seconds more. Remove the cooked gnocchi with a skimmer or slotted spoon and shake off the excess water.

In a nonstick skillet, heat the butter over medium heat. Sauté the boiled gnocchi for a few minutes until lightly browned.

To make the applesauce, place the maple syrup and apples in a small saucepan and bring to a boil while stirring. Once boiling, reduce the heat and simmer, covered, for 15 minutes. Serve the applesauce with the gnocchi as a dipping sauce.

DYP™ Chips

~~~~~~~~~~~~~~~~~~~~~~~ *makes 6 cups* ~~~~~~~~~~~~~~~~~~~~~~~

1 pound DYPs™

Salt or seasonings of choice

Peanut oil for frying

Heat about 2 inches of the oil in a large, high-sided pan to 375°F. Slice the
DYPs™ very thinly, about 1/16-inch thick, using a mandoline or food processor.
Working in batches, fry the DYPs™ in the hot oil for 2 to 3 minutes, or until
golden brown. Drain on paper towels and season immediately with salt or
other seasonings such as black pepper, Parmesan cheese, or fresh herbs. Serve
warm or at room temperature. These are best eaten the same day, but they can
be stored overnight in a container with the lid vented to prevent sogginess.

Tangy DYP™ & Onion Salad

makes 6 to 8 servings

3 pounds DYPs™, quartered

½ cup diced yellow onion

8 ounces cipollini onions, sliced in half horizontally

6 tablespoons (3 ounces) red wine vinegar

½ cup beef stock

4 tablespoons whole grain mustard

½ teaspoon salt

2 tablespoons minced chives

In a stockpot over high heat, cover the DYPs™ with cold water and bring to a boil. Cook 8 to 12 minutes or until the DYPs™ are fork tender. Drain and place in a large mixing bowl. Add the yellow onion and toss to combine.

In a medium saucepan, combine the cipollini onions, vinegar, and stock and bring to a boil over medium-high heat. Stir in the mustard and salt, and then pour the mixture over the DYPs™ and onions. Stir gently to coat. Sprinkle with the chives and serve at room temperature.

Chili DYP™ Skins

makes 4 to 6 servings

1 pound DYPs™

1 tablespoon vegetable oil

12 ounces ground turkey

1 medium onion, diced

1 red or green bell pepper, diced

1 garlic clove, minced

1 tablespoon chili powder

1 (14.5-ounce) can stewed tomatoes, undrained

1 (12-ounce) package Melissa's Steamed Ready-to-Eat Red Kidney Beans

¼ cup water

½ teaspoon salt

2 tablespoons shredded cheddar cheese

2 tablespoons sour cream

Preheat the oven to 425°F.

Place the DYPs™ on a baking sheet and roast for 12 to 15 minutes, or until fork tender.

Heat the oil in large nonstick skillet over medium-high heat. Add the ground turkey and cook, stirring to break up large pieces, about 5 minutes, or until the turkey is lightly browned. With a slotted spoon, remove the cooked turkey from the skillet and set aside.

Add the onion, bell pepper and garlic to the skillet. Cook until the vegetables are tender-crisp, about 4 to 5 minutes. Add the chili powder and continue to cook, stirring, for one minute more.

Stir in the turkey, kidney beans, stewed tomatoes, water, and salt and bring to a boil. Reduce the heat and simmer until the chili mixture is thickened, about 10 to 12 minutes.

Halve the DYPs™ lengthwise, cutting almost to the base. Mash the center of each one slightly with fork, leaving the skins intact. Spoon the chili mixture over each DYP™, dividing evenly. Top with the cheese and sour cream.

Hatch Chile DYP™ Salad

makes 8 to 10 servings

3 pounds DYPs™, cut in half

2 cloves garlic, chopped

4 tablespoons extra virgin olive oil, divided

Salt and freshly ground black pepper to taste

1 Melissa's perfect sweet onion, julienned

1 pound Melissa's Hatch Chiles, roasted, peeled, and chopped*

Vinaigrette:

1 cup seasoned rice vinegar

¼ cup granulated sugar

¼ pound Melissa's Hatch Chiles, roasted, peeled, and seeded*

1 clove garlic, chopped

Salt and freshly ground black pepper to taste

¾ cup olive oil

Place the DYPs™, garlic, and 3 tablespoons of the olive oil in a large bowl. Season with salt and pepper, and then toss to coat evenly. Spread evenly on a baking sheet and roast for 15 to 20 minutes, or until fork tender. Remove from the oven and let cool.

While the DYPs™ are baking, sauté the onion in the remaining tablespoon of oil over medium to medium-low heat, stirring occasionally, for 15 to 20 minutes, or until caramelized.

For the vinaigrette, combine all the ingredients except for the oil in a blender. With the motor running, slowly drizzle in the oil to emulsify. Taste and adjust the seasonings as needed.

To assemble the salad, place the DYPs™, caramelized onions, and the Hatch Chiles in a large mixing bowl, and toss gently to combine. Add the dressing, toss again, and serve.

*Hatch Chiles can be roasted over an open flame or under the broiler in an oven. The process typically takes about 8 minutes (less time for smaller chiles, more for larger).

To roast over an open flame on the stove: Use long-handled tongs to hold the chile over a medium flame, turning occasionally until evenly charred.

To roast over an open flame on a barbecue grill: This is the authentic traditional method and is the way our family prefers to roast our Hatch Chiles. Heat the grill until hot. Using long-handled tongs, turn the chiles over the direct heat until they are blackened and blistered all over.

To roast under the broiler: Preheat the broiler to high. Arrange the chiles in a single layer on a baking sheet and set under the broiler. Roast until blackened and blistered all over, turning occasionally.

Once roasted, choose one of our simple methods to cool and peel:

- Transfer the roasted chiles to a paper bag and roll the top down to close the bag.

- Transfer the roasted chiles to a pan and cover with a tight-fitting lid.

- Place the roasted chiles in a bowl and cover with a damp towel or with plastic wrap.

When the chiles are cool enough to handle, peel. You will find their skin peels off easily, revealing their silky flesh underneath. If you're not stuffing the chiles, remove and discard the stem and seeds. If you will be stuffing the chiles, leave the stem intact, cut a lengthwise slit up one side of each chile (don't cut through the tip end), and then delicately remove the seeds, being careful not to tear the chile. We recommend wearing plastic gloves when handling any chile.

Southwestern Salad

makes 6 to 8 servings

4 sprigs thyme

3 sprigs parsley

1 sprig rosemary

1 bay leaf

1 cup dry white wine

2 cloves garlic, minced

1½ pounds DYPs™, cut in half

1 tablespoon salt

2 stalks celery, thinly sliced

4 Melissa's Fire Roasted Sweet Red Bell Peppers, diced

3 ears corn, grilled and kernels removed

Dressing:

¼ cup white wine vinegar

1 tablespoon whole grain mustard

½ cup mayonnaise

2 chipotle peppers in adobo sauce, minced

2 teaspoons kosher salt

Freshly ground black pepper to taste

½ cup extra virgin olive oil

2 tablespoons minced parsley

2 green onions, thinly sliced

Tie the thyme, parsley, rosemary, and bay leaf together with a piece of kitchen twine. Place the bundle in a medium saucepan and add the wine, garlic, DYPs™, and salt. Add enough cold water so that the DYPs™ are covered by 1 inch. Bring to a boil over medium-high heat. Adjust the heat to maintain a gentle simmer and cook for 5 to 8 minutes, or until just fork tender. Drain and discard the herb bundle.

While the DYPs™ are cooking, make the dressing. Combine the vinegar, mustard, mayonnaise, chipotle peppers, salt, and black pepper in a large bowl. Gradually whisk in the oil to make a smooth dressing.

Add the warm DYPs™ to the dressing and toss gently to combine. Add the celery, red bell peppers, and grilled corn kernels, and toss gently to combine. When ready to serve, carefully fold in the parsley and green onions.

DYP™ Cobb Salad

makes 8 servings

2 pounds DYPs™

¾ teaspoon salt

8 cups mixed salad greens

2 large avocados

1 tablespoon fresh lemon juice

3 large tomatoes, seeded and diced

12 small green onions, sliced

2 cups (8 ounces) shredded sharp cheddar cheese

4 ounces blue cheese, crumbled

6 to 8 slices bacon, cooked and crumbled

Freshly ground black pepper to taste

Dressing:

6 ounces blue cheese, crumbled

½ cup Greek yogurt

3 tablespoons fresh lemon juice

2 tablespoons extra virgin olive oil

3 tablespoons milk

Salt and freshly ground black pepper to taste

In a large saucepan, cover the DYPs™ with cold water and bring to a boil over high heat. Cook for 8 to 12 minutes, or until fork tender, and then drain. When cool enough to handle, cut into quarters.

While the DYPs™ are boiling, prepare the dressing. Combine all the dressing ingredients in a small bowl. Pour half of the dressing over the warm DYPs™.

Arrange the salad greens evenly on a large serving platter. Halve, pit, and peel avocados, then cut into ½-inch cubes and toss with 1 tablespoon lemon juice.

Arrange the DYPs™, avocados, tomatoes, green onions, cheddar cheese, blue cheese, and bacon in rows over the salad greens. Season with black pepper. Serve with the remaining dressing.

DYP™ Bacon Salad

makes 6 to 8 servings

2 pounds DYPs™, cut in quarters

¼ teaspoon freshly ground black pepper

½ cup mayonnaise

½ cup Greek yogurt

8 ounces bacon, cooked and crumbled

6 green onions, chopped

2 celery ribs, finely chopped

5 Melissa's Pimientos Del Piquillo Peppers, drained and diced

¾ teaspoon salt

Paprika for garnish

In a large saucepan, cover the DYPs™ with cold water and bring to a boil over high heat. Cook 6 to 10 minutes, or until fork tender. Drain and let cool slightly.

In a large bowl, stir together the salt, pepper, mayonnaise, and Greek yogurt until well blended. Add the bacon, green onions, celery, piquillo peppers, and cooled DYPs™; toss gently to coat. Cover and chill at least 1 hour. Sprinkle lightly with paprika before serving.

Blue Cheese Grilled Salad

makes 6 servings

2 pounds DYPs™, cut in half

Cooking spray

Dressing:

½ cup vegetable oil

1 tablespoon chopped
fresh tarragon

1 tablespoon honey mustard

1 teaspoon lemon zest

2 tablespoons fresh lemon juice

1 teaspoon salt

½ teaspoon dried crushed
red pepper

4 ounces Gorgonzola, divided

Prepare a hot grill.

In a large saucepan, cover the DYPs™ with cold water and bring to a boil over high heat. Cook until just tender, about 7 to 11 minutes, and then drain.

Spray the DYPs™ with cooking spray and place on a hot grill. Cook for 10 minutes or until fully tender, turning occasionally.

While the DYPs™ are cooking, make the dressing. Whisk together all of the dressing ingredients except for half of the Gorgonzola. Gently toss with the grilled DYPs™. Place on a serving platter and sprinkle with the remaining cheese.

Gado Gado
(Indonesian Vegetable Salad)

~~~~~~~~~~~~~~~~~~~ *makes 4 servings* ~~~~~~~~~~~~~~~~~

Dressing:

½ cup creamy peanut butter

¾ cup coconut milk

2 teaspoons light soy sauce

1 tablespoon brown sugar

1 tablespoon fresh lime juice

½ teaspoon chile powder

⅓ cup vegetable oil

Salt and freshly ground black pepper to taste

Salad:

2 cups chopped Napa cabbage

1½ cups boiled and cubed DYPs™

1 cup cubed cucumber

1 cup cubed Roma tomatoes

1 package Melissa's Organic Tofu (Hawaiian style), cubed

2 eggs, hard boiled and cubed

¾ cup bean sprouts

½ cup chopped green onions

½ cup chopped fresh cilantro

½ cup chopped fresh mint

½ cup roasted peanuts

Whisk the dressing ingredients together and set aside.

On a large platter, place the cabbage in the center, and then place the DYPs™, cucumber, tomatoes, tofu, and hard boiled eggs around the edges. Sprinkle the bean sprouts, green onions, cilantro, mint, and peanuts over the cabbage. Season with salt and pepper. Serve with the dressing on the side for a nice presentation or, if preferred, toss together just before serving.

Baked DYP™ Pizza

~~~~~~~~~~~~~~ *makes 6 to 8 servings* ~~~~~~~~~~~~~~

Pizza Dough:

1 cup warm water

1 tablespoon honey

2½ teaspoons active dry yeast

2½ cups all-purpose flour

½ teaspoon sea salt

2 teaspoons Italian seasoning

2 tablespoons extra virgin olive oil

Canola oil, for drizzling

1 pound DYPs™, quartered

2 tablespoons olive oil

Salt and freshly ground black pepper to taste

½ cup sour cream

½ cup ranch dressing

6 slices bacon, cooked and crumbled

1½ cups shredded mozzarella cheese

½ cup shredded cheddar cheese

2 green onions, thinly sliced

In a small bowl, combine the warm water and honey, and then stir in the yeast. Let the mixture stand for 15 minutes.

In the bowl of a standing mixer fitted with a dough hook, combine the flour, sea salt, Italian seasoning, and olive oil. Gradually add the yeast mixture to the flour with the mixer running at medium speed. Continue kneading the dough until it is smooth and firm, about 5 to 6 minutes. Remove the dough from the mixing bowl, drizzle it with the canola oil and rub the oil over the dough to completely coat. Place the dough in a large bowl, and then cover it with plastic wrap or a dish towel. Place the bowl in a warm place and let rise for 20 minutes, or until the dough has doubled in size.

Preheat the oven to 425°F.

While the dough is rising, toss the DYPs™ with the 2 tablespoons olive oil in a medium size bowl. Season

with salt and pepper. Place on a baking sheet and roast for 9 to 12 minutes, or until tender. Remove the DYPs™ from the oven and reduce the oven temperature to 350°F.

Once the dough has risen, roll it out on a lightly floured surface to about ⅛-inch thick. Transfer the dough to a pizza stone or a baking sheet. Bake for 8 minutes.

Meanwhile, in a small bowl, stir together the sour cream and ranch dressing.

To assemble the pizza, spread the sour cream mixture over the partially baked pizza crust. Top with the DYPs™, bacon, cheese, and green onions. Return the pizza to the oven and bake for 12 to 15 minutes, or until the cheese is melted. Serve hot.

DYP™ BBQ Pizza

~~~~~~~~~~~~~~~~ *makes 6 to 8 servings* ~~~~~~~~~~~~~~~~

Pizza Dough:

1 cup warm water

1 tablespoon honey

2½ teaspoons active dry yeast

2½ cups all-purpose flour

½ teaspoon sea salt

2 teaspoons Italian seasoning

2 tablespoons extra virgin olive oil

Canola oil, for drizzling

8 ounces DYPs™, thinly sliced

2 tablespoons extra virgin olive oil

Salt and freshly ground black pepper to taste

2 quarts water

1 chicken breast

Cooking spray

½ cup barbecue sauce, divided

1 cup shredded mozzarella cheese

First, make the pizza dough. In a small bowl, combine the cup of warm water and honey, and then stir in the yeast. Let the mixture stand for 15 minutes.

In the bowl of a standing mixer fitted with a dough hook, combine the flour, sea salt, and Italian seasoning. Gradually add the yeast mixture and the olive oil to the flour with the mixer running at medium speed. Continue kneading the dough until it is smooth and firm, about 5 to 6 minutes. Remove the dough from the mixing bowl, drizzle it with the canola oil and rub the oil over the dough to completely coat. Place the dough in a large bowl, and cover it with plastic wrap or a dish towel. Place the bowl in a warm place and let rise for 20 minutes, or until the dough has doubled in size.

Preheat the oven to 425°F.

While the pizza dough is rising, mix the DYPs™ with the 2 tablespoons olive oil in a medium bowl. Season with salt and pepper. Place on a baking sheet and roast for 9 to 12 minutes, or until tender. Remove from the oven and reduce the temperature to 350°F.

Once the dough has risen, roll it out on a lightly floured surface to about ⅛-inch thick. Transfer the dough to a pizza stone or baking sheet. Bake for 8 minutes.

In a medium saucepan, pour enough water to cover one chicken breast. Bring to a boil, add the chicken breast, and reduce the heat. Simmer for 20 to 25 minutes, or until the chicken is cooked thoroughly. Remove the chicken from water and let cool slightly. Shred the chicken using 2 forks.

To assemble the pizza, spread half of the barbecue sauce over the partially baked crust. Lay the DYPs™, slightly overlapping, around the outer edge of the pizza, and top with the shredded chicken. Drizzle with the remaining barbecue sauce and top with the cheese. Return the pizza to the oven and bake for 12 minutes, or until the cheese melts.

Breakfast Tostada

makes 4 servings

Salsa:

2 tomatoes, diced

¼ cup diced onion

1 fresh jalapeño, finely diced

Salt to taste

Tostada:

4 large eggs

Salt and freshly ground
black pepper to taste

1 tablespoon unsalted butter

4 (8-inch) corn tortillas,
fried and drained

½ cup refried beans (canned
is fine), warmed

1 cup diced and cooked
DYPs™, warm

1 cup shredded iceberg lettuce

1 large sprig cilantro for garnish
(chopped or whole)

In a small bowl, combine the tomatoes, onion, and jalapeño. Season the
salsa with salt and set aside.

In a medium bowl, beat the eggs and season with salt and pepper.

In a medium skillet, melt the butter over medium heat. Add the beaten eggs
and cook, stirring, until thoroughly cooked.

To assemble the tostadas, spread a fried corn tortilla with the warmed
refried beans. Top with the warmed DYPs™, shredded lettuce, and
scrambled eggs, and then garnish with the cilantro. Serve with the salsa.

Ham Steak and DYP™ Eggs Benedict

makes 4 servings

1½ pounds DYPs™, shredded

½ onion, minced

2 cups panko breadcrumbs

11 eggs, divided

Pinch kosher salt

Pinch smoked paprika

Canola oil for frying

2 (1-pound) ham steaks

½ teaspoon white wine vinegar

Hollandaise Sauce:

4 egg yolks

Juice of ½ lemon

2 sticks (16 tablespoons) unsalted butter, melted

Pinch kosher salt

Pinch cayenne pepper

In a large bowl, combine the DYPs™, onion, breadcrumbs, 3 of the eggs, and a pinch each of salt and smoked paprika. Form the DYP™ mixture into 8 patties.

Fill a large skillet with ½ inch of the oil and set over medium-high heat until the oil is very hot but not smoking. Add the patties, in batches if necessary to prevent crowding, and cook until golden brown on both sides, 2 to 3 minutes per side. Drain the patties on paper towels and drain all but about 2 tablespoons of the oil from the pan. Add the ham steaks to the pan and cook, flipping once, until browned on both sides. Set aside.

Bring a medium pot of water to a boil. Stir in the vinegar, and then reduce the heat to a simmer. Crack one egg and gently add it to the simmering water. Simmer for about 2 to 2½ minutes, or until the egg is set. Carefully remove the egg with a slotted spoon and drain on paper towels. Repeat with the remaining eggs.

Next make the hollandaise sauce. Place a stainless steel bowl over the pot of simmering water. In the bowl, whisk together the 4 egg yolks and the lemon juice. Slowly whisk in the melted butter and continue whisking until the sauce is thickened and doubled in volume. Remove the sauce from the heat and stir in the salt and cayenne.

To serve, cut the ham steaks in half and place one half on each of 4 plates. Place 2 DYP™ patties on each plate and top them with 2 poached eggs. Ladle the sauce over the eggs and enjoy.

DYP™ Breakfast Pie

makes 6 to 8 servings

Cooking spray

8 ounces bacon, diced

¼ green bell pepper, diced

¼ red bell pepper, diced

1 small onion, chopped

8 large eggs, beaten

1 pound DYPs™, grated

2¾ cups shredded sharp cheddar cheese

½ teaspoon black pepper

Salt to taste

Preheat the oven to 350°F. Coat a pie dish (or 6 to 8 individual ramekins) with cooking spray.

In a medium skillet over medium heat, sauté the bacon, peppers, and onion until the bacon is cooked through and the vegetables are soft. Drain on paper towels.

In a large bowl, whisk the eggs and the shredded DYPs™, cheese, salt, and pepper. Stir in the bacon and vegetable mixture. Pour into the prepared pie dish and spread evenly. Bake for 45 minutes, or until the center is set and a knife inserted in the center comes out clean. (Bake 20 to 30 minutes for individual ramekins.)

Soyrizo Breakfast Wrap

makes 10 servings

1 teaspoon olive oil

1 package Melissa's Soyrizo

1½ cups diced DYPs™

1 bunch green onions, sliced

2 tablespoons chopped cilantro

3 eggs, beaten

1 cup shredded cheddar cheese

5 (10-inch) flour tortillas, warmed

Heat a large sauté pan over medium-high heat, and add the oil. Add the soyrizo and sauté, stirring occasionally, for about 5 minutes, or until lightly browned. Add the DYPs™ and cook for 5 to 8 more minutes, or until the DYPs™ are tender. Add the green onions and cilantro, and sauté, stirring occasionally, for 2 to 3 more minutes. Reduce the heat to medium. Add the eggs and cheese. Cook, stirring occasionally, until the eggs are firm but moist and the cheese has melted. Divide the egg mixture equally among the tortillas. Fold the short sides of the tortilla in and fold the bottom flap up, and then roll up the tortillas. Cut in half and serve.

Triple Smoke 50/50 Burger

1 pound lean ground beef

1 pound ground Italian sausage

2 chipotle chiles in adobo, minced

2 tablespoons
Worcestershire sauce

1 sweet onion,
cut into 4 thick slices

1 pound DYPs™,
cut into shoestrings

Canola oil for frying and brushing

2 teaspoons smoked paprika

Salt and freshly ground black
pepper to taste

8 slices apple-smoked bacon,
cooked

8 Hawaiian sweet hamburger buns

Condiments such as mayonnaise,
ketchup, mustard, etc. (optional)

Prepare a grill over medium-hot coals (medium for gas grills).

In a large bowl, combine the beef, sausage, chipotle, and Worcestershire sauce and season with salt and pepper. Form the mixture into 8 patties. Place the patties on the grill and cook for 5 to 6 minutes per side, or until the patties are completely cooked through.

While the burgers are cooking, brush the onion slices with the oil and place them on the grill. Cook, flipping once, until there are nice grill marks on both sides.

In a high-sided pan over medium heat, add 1 inch of the canola oil. Heat the oil until hot but not smoking. Fry the DYPs™ until golden brown and drain on paper towels. Season immediately with the paprika, salt and pepper.

To assemble the burgers, add the desired condiments to the buns. Top with the cooked patties, bacon, grilled onions, and a handful of the shoestring DYPs™. Place the bun tops on and enjoy.

DYP™ Tacos

2 pounds DYPs™

6 cloves garlic, peeled

½ cup milk

¼ cup grated Parmesan cheese

2 tablespoons butter

1 teaspoon salt

¼ teaspoon cumin

3 Hatch Chiles, roasted, peeled and chopped *(see page 95)*

30 corn tortillas

Peanut oil for frying

½ green cabbage, shredded

2 Roma tomatoes, seeded and finely chopped

2 tablespoons fresh lime juice

½ teaspoon salt

Your favorite red or green tomatillo salsa

In a large saucepan, cover the DYPs™ and garlic with cold water and bring to a boil over high heat. Simmer 8 to 12 minutes, or until the DYPs™ are fork tender. Drain. Chop the garlic finely. In a large bowl, mash together the DYPs™, chopped garlic, milk, cheese, butter, salt, cumin, and Hatch Chiles.

Wrap the tortillas in a dish towel. Microwave for 1 minute to warm and soften tortillas.

Place a large spoonful (about ¼ cup) of DYP™ mixture in the center of a tortilla and fold over in half. In a large skillet, pour enough oil to come 1 inch up the sides. Heat the oil over medium to medium-high heat. Pan-fry the tacos a few at a time, being sure not to crowd the skillet, and turn the tacos once. Fry until crispy and lightly browned on both sides. Repeat for the remaining tacos, adding more oil if needed.

In a medium bowl, combine the cabbage, tomato, lime juice, and salt. Serve the tacos garnished with the cabbage mixture and your favorite salsa.

Note: *This recipe can be easily halved for 15 tacos.*

Chicken "Po Ticos" (Taquitos)

makes 18 taquitos

4 cups cooked, shredded chicken

1 cup cooked, mashed DYPs™

½ cup shredded cheddar cheese

½ cooked, chopped onion

⅓ cup roasted, chopped Hatch Chiles *(see page 95)*

18 corn tortillas

Canola oil for frying

Combine the chicken, mashed DYPs™, cheese, onion, and chiles in a medium bowl.

Heat tortillas 6 at a time, wrapped in paper towel, for 1 minute in the microwave.

Place ¼ cup of the filling in each tortilla toward the edge, and then, starting at that end, roll the tortillas tightly and secure with a toothpick. Repeat with the remaining tortillas and filling.

In a medium skillet, heat 1 inch of oil to 350°F, just before it starts to smoke. Add a few taquitos at a time without crowding the skillet. Fry for 3 to 4 minutes, or until the tortillas are crispy and golden brown.

Grilled Rib-eyes *with* Broccoli-DYP™ Mash

~~~~~~~~~~~~~~~~~~~~ *makes 2 to 4 servings* ~~~~~~~~~~~~~~~~~~~~

Rib-eye Rub:

1 tablespoon kosher salt

1 tablespoon freshly ground black pepper

1 tablespoon smoked paprika

1 tablespoon brown sugar

2 (1.25-pound) bone-in rib-eye steaks

2 pounds DYPs™, cut in half

1 pound fresh broccoli, trimmed and cut into florets

¼ cup heavy cream

¼ cup milk

3 tablespoons unsalted butter, divided

Kosher salt and freshly ground black pepper to taste

2 tablespoons cornstarch

2 cups beef broth

2 cups red wine

~~~~~~

To make the rub, combine the salt, pepper, smoked paprika, and brown sugar in a small bowl. Rub the mixture onto both sides of the steaks. Let the steaks rest for 30 minutes.

Place the DYPs™ and broccoli florets in a large saucepan. Cover with cold water and bring to a boil. Reduce the heat and simmer for 20 minutes, or until the vegetables are tender. Drain the vegetables and place them in the bowl of a standing mixer.

Place the cream, milk, and 2 tablespoons of the butter in a small saucepan over medium heat. When the mixture is hot, stir into the DYPs™ and season with salt and pepper. Cover the bowl with foil to keep warm.

Pre-heat a grill to high heat. When hot, grill the steaks for 4 to 6 minutes on each side for medium-rare, or longer for well-done steaks.

In a small bowl, whisk together the cornstarch and ½ cup of the broth. In a medium sauce pot, add the remaining 1½ cups broth and the wine and bring to a boil. Stir in the cornstarch mixture and simmer, stirring often, about 10 to 12 minutes, or until thickened. Stir in the remaining tablespoon of butter, and then season to taste with more salt and smoked paprika.

To serve, place some of the mashed vegetables on a plate. Place a steak on the plate slightly overlapping the vegetables and top with some of the sauce.

Grilled Shrimp
with Lemon-DYP™ Sauce

~~~~~~~~~~~~~~~~~~~~ *makes 4 servings* ~~~~~~~~~~~~~~~~~~~~

1 pound fresh shrimp,
peeled and deveined

Juice of 2 limes

1 tablespoon Melissa's
Pico de Gallo Seasoning

1 pound DYPs™

Juice of 2 lemons

3 cloves garlic, minced or run
through a garlic press

½ cup extra virgin olive oil

Salt and freshly ground black
pepper to taste

~~~~~~

Place the shrimp in a bowl with the lime juice and pico de gallo seasoning.
Gently stir and set aside.

Place the DYPs™ in a large saucepan. Cover with cold water and bring to a
boil. Reduce the heat and cook for 5 to 8 minutes, or until fork tender. Drain,
saving ¼ cup of the boiled water. Press the DYPs™ through a ricer into a mixing
bowl. Add the lemon juice and garlic, and then stir in the olive oil and reserved
cooking water. Season the sauce with salt and pepper to taste.

Prepare a hot grill over
medium-high heat. Cook
the shrimp until opaque
and cooked through,
about 2 minutes per side.
Serve with the DYP™
sauce and enjoy.

Almond DYPs™

makes 20 to 24 appetizers

1½ pounds DYPs™

¾ cup sour cream

Salt to taste

Slivered almonds for topping

Chopped fresh dill, for garnish

In a large saucepan, cover the DYPs™ with cold water and bring to a boil over high heat. Cook until fork tender, about 6 to 9 minutes. Drain and cool.

Slice off the bottom end of each DYP™ (so that it can sit upright). Slice off a third of the top and discard (or eat). If the DYPs™ are medium size, then cut them in half and use both halves. With a melon baller, scoop out their centers. Mash the DYP™ centers with the sour cream and season with salt to taste. Fill the DYP™ shells with the mashed DYPs™. Top with slivered almonds and garnish with the dill.

Angelina's Gorditas

makes 10 servings

1 pound ground beef

8 ounces DYPs™, diced small

½ cup water

1½ teaspoons salt, divided

½ teaspoon freshly ground black pepper

½ teaspoon onion powder

½ teaspoon garlic powder

1 tablespoon ground cumin

2 cups corn masa harina

½ cup cooked and mashed DYPs™

¼ cup shredded cheddar cheese

2 cups warm water

Canola oil for frying

Shredded lettuce, chopped tomato, shredded cheddar cheese, and tomato salsa for garnish

In a medium sauce pan over medium-high heat, brown the ground beef. Drain the excess fat and discard. Add the DYPs™, water, ½ teaspoon of salt, pepper, onion powder, garlic powder, and cumin to the ground beef. Reduce heat, cover, and cook until the DYPs™ are very soft, about 10 to 12 minutes.

In a medium bowl combine the masa harina, mashed DYPs™, cheese and remaining 1 teaspoon of salt. Using clean hands, mix the warm water into the masa ¼ cup at a time. Add water and knead until the dough forms into a ball. Divide the dough into 10 equal-size balls. Pat each ball into a gordita patty ½-inch thick.

In a deep, heavy medium skillet or saucepan, heat 1 inch of the oil over medium to medium-high heat. When the oil is hot enough to make the edge of a gordita sizzle sharply, or about 350°F on a deep-fry thermometer, start frying the gorditas. Add the gorditas, three at a time, to the hot oil. Cook for about 15 seconds, and then flip them over. Cook about 5 minutes, or until the gorditas are nicely crisp and golden brown. When they're ready, most will have puffed up a little, like pita bread. Drain on paper towels.

Once all of the gorditas are fried, use a small knife to cut a slit in the thin edge of each one about halfway around its circumference, opening a pocket. As you cut them, fill each gordita with about ¼ cup of the meat mixture, and then garnish with lettuce, tomato, and cheese. Serve with the salsa.

Grilled DYP™ Skewers
with Shallots

~~~~~~~~~~~~~~~~~ *makes 6 servings* ~~~~~~~~~~~~~~~~~

2 pounds DYPs™

1 pound shallots, cut in half

2 tablespoons olive oil

Salt to taste

~~~~~~

Preheat a grill to medium-high heat.

Place the DYPs™ in a large saucepan. Cover with cold water and bring to a boil. Reduce the heat and cook for 8 minutes, or until just tender, and then drain.

Thread the DYPs™ onto a metal skewer, alternating with the shallot halves. Brush the skewers with the oil and season with the salt.

Grill, turning occasionally, for 10 to 12 minutes, or until the DYPs™ are tender.

Lightly Seasoned DYP™ Skewers

makes 18 to 20 skewers

1 pound DYPs™, cut in half

1 pint heirloom baby tomatoes

24 whole Melissa's Pearl Onions, peeled

2 tablespoons olive oil

1½ teaspoons dried thyme

Salt and freshly ground black pepper to taste

Preheat the broiler or a grill to medium-high heat.

In a large saucepan, cover the DYPs™ with cold water and bring to a boil over high heat. Cook about 4 to 7 minutes or until just tender, and then drain. Arrange the cooked DYPs™, tomatoes, and onions alternately on skewers. In a small bowl, combine the olive oil, thyme, salt, and pepper, and brush onto the skewered vegetables. Broil or grill the skewers for 12 minutes, turning occasionally, or until the edges of the DYPs™ are golden brown.

Jimmy's Virginia DYPs™

makes 4 to 6 servings

2 pounds DYPs™, quartered

2 large shallots, thinly sliced

½ cup cider vinegar

1 tablespoon extra-virgin olive oil

1 teaspoon salt

Freshly ground black pepper

In a large saucepan, cover the DYPs™ with cold water and bring to a boil over high heat. Cook until fork tender, about 6 to 10 minutes, and then drain.

Mix the DYPs™ with the shallots. Season with vinegar, oil, salt, and a good amount of pepper, and toss to coat evenly. Serve at room temperature.

Tex-Mex DYP™ Mash

makes 6 to 8 servings

2 pounds DYPs™

Salt

1¼ cups buttermilk, warmed

4 tablespoons (¼ cup) butter, melted

½ teaspoon freshly ground black pepper

3 Hatch Chiles, roasted, peeled, and chopped *(see page 95)*

1 cup shredded cheddar cheese

Preheat the oven to 350°F.

In a large saucepan, cover the DYPs™ with cold, salted water and bring to a boil over high heat. Cook 8 to 12 minutes, or until fork tender. Drain and then mash with a potato masher to your desired consistency.

Stir in the warm buttermilk, melted butter, black pepper, chiles, and cheese. Taste and adjust the seasoning with salt and pepper if needed, and stir to blend.

Spoon the mixture into a lightly greased 2½-quart baking dish or 8 (10-ounce) ramekins. Bake for 35 minutes, and then serve.

Honey-Grilled Vegetables

makes 4 to 6 servings

1 pound DYPs™, cut in half

¼ cup honey

3 tablespoons dry white wine

1 clove garlic, minced

1 teaspoon crushed dried thyme leaves

½ teaspoon salt

½ teaspoon freshly ground black pepper

2 zucchini, halved lengthwise

1 medium eggplant, cut into ½-inch-thick slices

1 green bell pepper, halved and seeded

1 red bell pepper, halved and seeded

1 large onion, cut into wedges

Prepare a hot grill or preheat the oven to 400°F.

In a large saucepan, cover the DYPs™ with cold water and bring to a boil over high heat. Simmer 4 to 7 minutes, or until fork tender. Drain.

Combine the honey, wine, garlic, thyme, salt, and pepper in small bowl; mix well. Place the DYPs™ and the remaining vegetables on oiled grill over hot coals or high heat. Grill 20 to 25 minutes, turning and brushing with honey mixture every 7 to 8 minutes, until the vegetables are slightly charred and softened.

Alternatively, place the vegetables on a baking sheet and roast for 25 minutes, or until tender, stirring every 8 to 10 minutes to prevent burning.

DUTCH YELLOW® POTATOES

FALL

Mediterranean Butternut Soup

makes 6 to 8 servings

1 tablespoon olive oil

1 medium onion, diced

2 cloves garlic, minced

½ teaspoon saffron threads

6 cups vegetable broth, divided

1 Roma tomato, diced

1 butternut squash, peeled, seeded, and diced into ½-inch pieces

1 pound DYPs™, cut in half

1 canela (cinnamon) stick

2 teaspoons ground cumin

1 (15-ounce) can garbanzo beans

Salt and freshly ground black pepper to taste

½ cup chopped cilantro

Heat the oil in a heavy, large pot over medium heat. Add the onion and sauté until tender, 2 to 3 minutes. Add the garlic and saffron and stir 1 minute. Add 5 cups of the broth, then the tomato, squash, DYPs™, canela stick, and cumin. Increase the heat to high and bring to a boil. Reduce the heat, cover, and simmer until the vegetables are very tender, about 20 minutes. Stir in the garbanzo beans and simmer 5 minutes more. Season with salt and pepper. Ladle the soup into bowls, sprinkle with the cilantro, and serve.

DYP™ and Leek Soup

makes 6 servings

1½ cups DYPs™, diced small

1 package Melissa's Belgian Style Leeks, sliced lengthwise, then cut crosswise into 1-inch pieces (about 2 leeks)

2 tablespoons butter

2 cups water

2 cups vegetable or chicken broth, plus more for thinning

¾ teaspoon sea salt

White pepper to taste

3 slices thick cut bacon, cooked and crumbled

Place the DYPs™ in a bowl and cover with water to prevent discoloration.

Set a large stock pot over low heat and add the butter. Add the leeks and cook, stirring occasionally, until softened. Drain the DYPs™ and add them to the leeks, along with 2 cups fresh water, the broth, sea salt, and white pepper. Increase the heat to high and bring to a boil. Cover and reduce the heat to a simmer. Cook for 30 minutes, or until the DYPs™ are very soft.

Pour the soup mixture into a blender, in batches if needed, and purée until smooth. (Be careful with hot liquids and blenders!) Return the puréed soup to the pan and add broth to reach the desired consistency. Continue to cook over low heat until heated thoroughly.

Serve in individual bowls topped with the crumbled bacon.

Aunt Marie's DYP™
and Fava Bean Soup

~~~~~ *makes 6 to 8 servings* ~~~~~

2 tablespoons olive oil

4 stalks celery, trimmed and diced

½ large onion, diced

2 teaspoons ground turmeric

1 pound DYPs™, quartered

5 cups vegetable broth

Kosher salt and freshly ground black pepper to taste

3 pinches saffron

1 (12.3-ounce) package Melissa's Fava Beans (Steamed), rinsed

2 tablespoons chopped cilantro or flat leaf parsley

Heat the oil in a large stockpot over medium heat until it begins to sizzle. Add the celery, onion, and turmeric and stir to combine. Sauté over medium heat, stirring often, for about 2 to 3 minutes, or until the onion is translucent. Add the DYPs™ and sauté for 1 minute. Add the vegetable broth, salt, pepper, and saffron. Bring to a low boil and cook until the DYPs™ are tender, about 3 to 6 minutes. Add the fava beans and season with salt and pepper to taste. Cook for another 2 to 3 minutes, or until the fava beans are heated through.

Using a slotted spoon, remove about half the vegetables from the pot into a bowl. Mash them using a fork or potato masher, and then return them to the pot. Stir in the cilantro or parsley.

DYP™ and Grilled Shrimp Soup

makes 8 to 10 servings

1 pound large shrimp, peeled and deveined

Salt, freshly ground black pepper, and Melissa's Pico de Gallo Seasoning to taste

2 tablespoons extra virgin olive oil

2 tablespoons unsalted butter

1 sweet onion, diced

2 carrots, trimmed and sliced

2 stalks celery, trimmed and sliced

2 (14.5-ounce) cans stewed tomatoes

¼ cup sherry

4 cups chicken broth

2 ears fresh corn, husks and silks removed, cut into 1-inch rounds

1 pound DYPs™, diced

Prepare a hot grill.

Season the shrimp with the salt, pepper, and pico de gallo seasoning. Grill until opaque, about 2 minutes per side. Set aside.

Add the oil and butter to a large stock pot over medium heat. When the butter is melted, add the onion, carrots, and celery and sauté, stirring often, for 5 minutes, or until the onion is softened and translucent. Add the tomatoes (with their juice) and the sherry and cook for 5 minutes more. Add the broth, corn, and DYPs™. Bring to a boil, then reduce the heat and simmer for 30 minutes, or until the DYPs™ are tender and the flavors have melded. Add the shrimp and simmer for 2 minutes. Serve hot.

Red Bell Pepper Soup

serves 6 to 8

2 tablespoons olive oil

1 sweet onion, peeled and roughly chopped

3 whole thyme sprigs

Pinch of salt

Pinch of freshly ground black pepper

2 cloves garlic, minced

4 cups chicken broth

5 ounces evaporated milk

1 pound DYPs™, cut into quarters

1 (15.5-ounce) jar Melissa's Fire Roasted Sweet Red Bell Peppers, drained

Set a large stockpot over medium heat and add the oil. Add the onions and thyme sprigs and season with salt and pepper. Sauté for 5 minutes, stirring often. When the onions are translucent, add the garlic and let cook until fragrant but not browned. Add the chicken broth, evaporated milk, DYPs™, and roasted peppers. Increase the heat to high and bring to a boil. Reduce the heat to a simmer and cook for 20 minutes, or until DYPs™ are fork tender.

Remove the thyme sprigs and carefully purée the soup with a handheld immersion blender, in a food processor, or in a blender. (Be careful with hot liquids and blenders!) Serve hot.

Holiday Soup

makes 8 to 10 servings

2 tablespoons extra virgin olive oil

2 large yellow onions, chopped into large pieces

1 shallot, minced

2 green onions with tops, chopped

3 cloves peeled garlic, minced

1 jalapeño chile, minced

1½ tablespoons all-purpose flour

1 dried bay leaf

⅓ cup white wine

3 pounds DYPs™, cut in half

6 cups low-sodium chicken broth

½ teaspoon each salt and freshly ground black pepper

Heat the olive oil in a Dutch oven over medium-high heat. Add the yellow onions, shallot, green onions, garlic, and jalapeño and cook until the onions are translucent, stirring often, about 5 minutes. Sprinkle in the flour and add the bay leaf and stir well. Let cook a minute or two until the flour is pale gold.

Add the wine and increase the heat to high. Stir the mixture, making sure to scrape all of the bits from the bottom of the pot. Cook until almost all of the liquid has evaporated.

Add the DYPs™, broth, salt, and pepper, and bring the remaining liquid to a boil. Reduce the heat to a simmer, cover, and cook for 45 minutes or until the DYPs™ are fork tender.

Remove and discard the bay leaf. Remove 2 cups of the soup from the pot and purée it in a blender. (Be careful with hot liquids and blenders!) Add the puréed mixture back to the soup pot and mix well. Serve hot.

Hot DYP™ Salad

2 pounds DYPs™

1 cup finely chopped celery

2 teaspoons finely chopped parsley

½ onion, chopped

4 tablespoons salad oil

4 tablespoons vinegar

1 teaspoon salt

½ teaspoon freshly ground black pepper

½ teaspoon paprika

Preheat the oven to 350°F.

Place the DYPs™ in a large saucepan. Cover with cold, salted water and bring to a boil. Reduce the heat and cook for about 8 to 12 minutes, or until fork tender; drain. Slice the DYPs™ thinly. Place the slices in a buttered baking dish and top with the celery, parsley, and onion.

In a small bowl, combine the oil, vinegar, salt, pepper, and paprika. Pour the oil mixture over the vegetables. Cover the baking dish with foil and bake for about 15 minutes to heat thoroughly. Serve warm.

DYP™ and Tuna Salad

makes 4 to 6 servings

⅓ cup extra virgin olive oil

3 tablespoons sherry vinegar

1 tablespoon Dijon mustard

1 tablespoon chopped fresh thyme

1 tablespoon chopped
fresh rosemary

1½ pounds DYPs™,
boiled and quartered

2 Roma tomatoes, diced

2 (5.1-ounce) cans good-quality
tuna, drained

½ red onion, diced small

6 hard-boiled eggs, quartered

In a bowl, whisk together the oil, vinegar, mustard, thyme, and rosemary.

In another bowl, gently combine the DYPs™, tomatoes, tuna, and onion. Add the dressing and mix gently. Transfer the mixture to a platter and arrange the eggs on top. The mixture can also be served in lettuce cups.

DYP™, Fig, *and* Tarragon Salad

makes 6 to 8 servings

1½ pounds DYPs™, quartered

1 dried bay leaf

2 cloves garlic, finely chopped

Salt and freshly ground black pepper to taste

1 teaspoon Dijon mustard

3 tablespoons red wine vinegar

½ cup extra virgin olive oil

1 stalk celery, trimmed and cut into ¼-inch dice

12 dried Calimyrna figs, stems removed, cut lengthwise into quarters

½ small red onion, cut into ¼-inch dice

2 tablespoons chopped Italian parsley

1 tablespoon chopped tarragon

¼ cup green olives, pitted and chopped

Place the DYPs™ in a large saucepan. Cover with cold water and add the bay leaf and garlic. Season with salt and pepper and bring to a boil. Reduce the heat and cook for 4 to 7 minutes, or until fork tender. Drain the DYPs™ and discard the bay leaf.

Whisk the mustard and red wine vinegar together in a small bowl. Continue whisking while slowly adding the olive oil in a thin, steady stream. Season the vinaigrette with salt and pepper to taste.

Just before serving, combine the DYPs™, celery, figs, red onion, parsley, tarragon, and green olives in a large bowl. Add the vinaigrette and toss to coat. Season with salt and pepper if necessary and serve.

Creamy Smashed DYPs™

~~~~~~~~~~~~~~~~~~~~~~~~~~~ *makes 6 servings* ~~~~~~~~~~~~~~~~~~~~~~~~~~~

2 pounds DYPs™

¼ cup chopped green onions

¾ cup Greek yogurt

Sea salt to taste

Place the DYPs™ in a large saucepan. Cover with lightly salted cold water and bring to a boil. Reduce the heat and simmer for 8 to 12 minutes, or until fork tender; drain.

Using a potato masher, smash the DYPs™ to desired consistency. Stir in the chopped green onions and Greek yogurt, and then season to taste with sea salt.

Carrot and DYP™ Purée

makes 8 servings

2 pounds DYPs™, quartered

½ pound Melissa's Organic Peeled Baby Carrots, cut into chunks

½ cup crème fraîche or sour cream

6 tablespoons (3 ounces) unsalted butter

1 tablespoon sweet mustard

Salt and freshly ground black pepper to taste

Place the DYPs™ and carrots in a large saucepan. Cover with cold water and bring to a boil. Reduce the heat and cook for about 12 to 15 minutes, or until the vegetables are fork tender. Drain, reserving 2 cups of the cooking liquid.

Purée the vegetables in a food mill or ricer or using a potato masher, adding some of the cooking liquid if necessary to reach a smooth consistency.

Transfer the purée back into the saucepan over low heat. Stir in the crème fraîche, butter, and mustard and heat through. Season with salt and pepper to taste.

DYP™, Parsnip, *and* Carrot Purée

~~~~~~ *makes 6 servings* ~~~~~~

1½ pounds DYPs™, cut in half

8 ounces Melissa's Sweet Baby Carrots, cut into 1-inch pieces

8 ounces parsnips, peeled and cut into 1-inch pieces

½ cup Greek yogurt

4 tablespoons unsalted butter

1½ tablespoons Melissa's Cream Style Horseradish

Salt to taste

White pepper to taste

Place the DYPs™, carrots, and parsnips in a large saucepan. Cover with cold water and bring to a boil. Reduce the heat and simmer for about 15 minutes or until all the vegetables are fork tender. Drain, reserving some of the liquid.

Pass the vegetables through a food mill or potato ricer, adding some of the liquid if necessary to reach a purée consistency.

Transfer the vegetable purée to a large saucepan. Add the Greek yogurt, butter, and horseradish. Season with salt and white pepper and reheat slowly over low heat.

Lemon DYP™ Fans

makes 4 servings

1 pound DYPs™

¼ cup grated Parmesan cheese

3 tablespoons chopped
fresh parsley

½ teaspoon paprika

¼ teaspoon salt

¼ cup margarine

1 tablespoon fresh lemon juice

2 teaspoons grated lemon zest

Preheat the oven to 400°F.

Partially cut each DYP™ crosswise into ¼-inch thick slices, almost through to bottom, but keeping the slices attached.

Combine the Parmesan, parsley, paprika, and salt in a small bowl and set aside. In a microwave-safe glass measuring cup, combine the margarine, lemon juice and lemon zest. Microwave, uncovered, on high for 30 to 40 seconds, or until the margarine is melted.

Arrange the DYPs™, cut-side up, in a baking dish. Brush the tops and sides of the DYPs™ with the margarine mixture. Cover with foil and bake, brushing with the remaining margarine mixture half way through cooking, for 30 to 35 minutes, or until the DYPs™ are tender. Sprinkle the DYPs™ with the Parmesan mixture. Cover and let stand for 5 minutes to melt the cheese.

Spanish Tortilla

makes 8 servings

1 cup olive oil

1½ pounds DYPs™, thinly sliced

1 medium onion, thinly sliced

Salt and freshly ground black pepper to taste

6 extra-large or jumbo eggs

Heat the oil in a 10-inch nonstick skillet over medium heat. Add the DYPs™ and onions and season with salt and pepper. Cook, gently stirring occasionally, until the DYPs™ are tender when pierced with a small knife, about 2 to 4 minutes. Adjust the heat so they do not brown.

Meanwhile, in a large bowl, beat the eggs with salt and pepper.

Drain the DYPs™ and onions in a colander, reserving the oil. Gently stir the DYPs™ and onions into the egg mixture.

Pour any extra oil out of the skillet and reserve. Heat the skillet over medium heat for one minute. Add 2 tablespoons of the oil back to the skillet and then add the egg and DYP™ mixture without stirring. As soon as the edges firm up, after a minute or so, reduce the heat to medium-low. Cook 5 minutes more.

Insert a rubber spatula all around the edges of the tortilla to make sure it will slide from the pan. The top will still be a bit runny. Carefully slide the tortilla out onto a plate. Cover the tortilla with another plate, and then, holding the plates tightly, invert them. Add 1 tablespoon of the reserved oil back to the skillet, and then use the spatula to coax the tortilla, runny-side down, back into the pan. Cook for 5 minutes, or until the eggs are set all the way through. Slide the tortilla from the skillet onto a clean plate. Cover loosely with foil and let set for 15 minutes to firm up. Cut the tortilla into wedges for a side dish or into bite-sized cubes for appetizers. Serve warm or at room temperature.

Rosemary DYP™ Wedges

makes 6 to 8 servings

1½ pounds DYPs™

4 tablespoons (¼ cup) unsalted butter, melted, divided

2 teaspoons finely chopped fresh rosemary

Salt and freshly ground black pepper to taste

Cooking spray (optional)

Preheat the oven to 425°F.

Using a mandoline or a food processor fitted with the slicing blade, slice the DYPs™ very thinly.

Brush the bottom and sides of a 9-inch heavy ovenproof skillet, preferably nonstick, with some of the butter. Arrange the DYP™ slices in layers in the skillet, overlapping them slightly. Sprinkle with salt and pepper and some of the rosemary. As you go, brush each new layer with butter and sprinkle with salt, pepper and rosemary.

Butter or lightly coat with cooking spray one side of a sheet of foil. Place coated-side down on top of the DYPs™ and press down on the layers firmly. Bake in the middle of the oven for 30 minutes.

Remove the foil and bake the DYP™ cake for 25 to 30 minutes more, or until the DYP™ slices are tender and golden.

Invert the DYP™ cake onto a cutting board and cut it into 8 wedges.

Escalloped DYPs™

makes 8 servings

3 tablespoons unsalted butter

3 tablespoons flour

2 cups milk

Pinch of cayenne pepper

1½ pounds DYPs™,
cut into ¼-inch thick slices

1 cup chopped yellow onion
(about ½ large onion)

½ teaspoon salt

½ teaspoon freshly ground
black pepper

4 cups shredded sharp
cheddar cheese

Preheat the oven to 375°F.

Melt the butter in a heavy saucepan over low heat. Add the flour, stirring until smooth. Cook 1 minute, stirring constantly, until the mixture is light golden. Gradually stir in the milk and cayenne. Cook over medium heat, stirring constantly, until thickened and bubbly. Keep warm, but do not allow to scorch.

In a 2-quart casserole dish, place half of the DYP™ slices in one layer. Top with half the onion, salt, pepper, cheese, and cream sauce, then repeat. Cover the dish with foil and place on a large cookie sheet to prevent oven spills. Bake for 45 minutes. Remove the foil cover and continue baking about 15 to 20 minutes more, or until the DYPs™ are fork tender.

DYP™ Blintzes

makes 10 to 12 blintzes

1 tablespoon extra virgin olive oil

1 tablespoon unsalted butter

1 large onion, thinly sliced

1 pinch granulated sugar

½ teaspoon salt

½ teaspoon freshly ground black pepper

1½ pounds DYPs™

¼ cup whole milk

1 package Melissa's Egg Roll Wraps

1 egg white, lightly beaten

Vegetable oil for frying

Sour cream or Greek yogurt (optional)

In a medium skillet, heat the olive oil and butter over medium heat. Add the onion and sugar and season with salt and pepper. Cook, stirring occasionally, until caramelized, about 20 minutes.

Meanwhile, place the DYPs™ in a microwave-safe dish. Cook on high for about 10 minutes or until fork tender. Add the milk, and mash until almost smooth, leaving a little texture. Stir in the caramelized onions and add salt and pepper if needed.

Divide the filling evenly on the centers of 14 egg roll wraps. Brush the edges with the egg white, fold in the sides, and roll them as you would a burrito, making sure that the ends are closed and sealed. Pour ½ inch of the vegetable oil into a frying pan and heat over medium heat. Fry the blintzes until golden brown on all sides. Drain them on paper towels. To serve, place the blintzes on a serving platter and garnish with sour cream or Greek yogurt.

Eric's Root Vegetable Pot Stickers

makes about 40 pot stickers

2 large carrots

1 golden beet, peeled

4 large DYPs™

¼ cup sliced green onion (green parts only)

2 tablespoons grated fresh ginger

1 teaspoon soy sauce

Pinch of salt

1 (14-ounce) package Melissa's Wonton Wrappers

1 tablespoon vegetable oil, or more if needed

¼ cup water, or more if needed.

Grate the carrots, beet, and DYPs™ with a large Microplane grater. In a large bowl, combine the grated vegetables, green onion, ginger, soy sauce, and salt, and mix well.

To assemble, place one tablespoon of the mixture in the center of a wonton wrapper. Dip your finger in a bowl of water and wet the edges of the wonton wrapper. Bring two opposite corners together, and then bring the other two corners up, to make a little purse. Pinch firmly to seal the seams. Place the completed pot stickers on a baking sheet until all are assembled. (The potstickers can be frozen at this stage on a sheet pan, and then transferred to a resealable plastic bag once frozen. To cook, follow the instructions below and add a 2 or 3 minutes of steaming time.)

To cook, set a large sauté pan over medium high heat and add the vegetable oil. When the oil is hot, place the pot stickers in the pan, being sure to not crowd the pan. (If necessary, cook in batches.)

Let cook until golden brown on the bottom, about 2 minutes, and then pour ¼ cup of water into the pan and cover with a lid. Let the pot stickers steam until the water has evaporated and they are warmed throughout. Repeat the process for any additional batches.

Serve with a homemade or store bought dumpling sauce for dipping.

Eric's DYP™–Shiitake Pot Stickers

~~~~~~~~~~~~ *makes about 25 pot stickers* ~~~~~~~~~~~~

2 tablespoon vegetable oil

12 fresh shiitake mushrooms, diced

¼ cup sliced green onion (green parts only)

4 large DYPs™, shredded

2 tablespoons grated fresh ginger

1 teaspoon soy sauce

Pinch of salt

1 (14-ounce) package Melissa's Wonton Wrappers

¼ cup water

~~~~~~~~~~~~~~~~~~~~~~~~~~~~~~

Set a medium saucepan over medium-high heat. When hot, add 1 tablespoon of the oil and sauté the mushrooms until they've just released their liquid and are starting to brown.

In a large bowl, combine the mushrooms, green onion, DYPs™, ginger, soy sauce, and salt, and mix well.

To assemble, place one tablespoon of the mixture in the center of a wonton wrapper. Dip your finger in a bowl of water and wet the edges of the wonton wrapper. Bring two opposite corners together, and then bring the other two corners up, to make a little purse. Pinch firmly to seal the seams. Place the completed pot stickers on a baking sheet until all are assembled. (The potstickers can be frozen at this stage on a sheet pan, and then transferred to a resealable plastic bag once frozen. To cook, follow the instructions below and add a 2 or 3 minutes of steaming time.)

To cook, set a large sauté pan over medium high heat and add the vegetable oil. When the oil is hot, place the pot stickers in the pan, being sure to not crowd the pan. (If necessary, cook in batches.) Let cook until golden brown on the bottom, about 2 minutes, and then pour ¼ cup of water into the pan and cover with a lid. Let the pot stickers steam until the water has evaporated and they are warmed throughout. Repeat the process for any additional batches.

Serve with a homemade or store bought dumpling sauce for dipping.

Eric's Fennel, Veal, and DYP™ Pot Stickers

makes about 40 pot stickers

1 large fennel bulb with fronds

1 pound ground veal

4 large DYPs™, shredded

½ teaspoon fish sauce

Pinch of salt

1 (14-ounce) package Melissa's Wonton Wrappers

1 tablespoon vegetable oil

¼ cup water

Finely chop the fennel bulb, being sure to remove the core, and mince the fennel fronds. In a large bowl, gently combine the ground veal, fennel, fennel fronds, DYPs™, fish sauce, and salt, until just mixed.

To assemble, place one tablespoon of the mixture in the center of a wonton wrapper. Dip your finger in a bowl of water and wet the edges of the wonton wrapper. Bring two opposite corners together, and then bring the other two corners up, to make a little purse. Pinch firmly to seal the seams. Place the completed pot stickers on a baking sheet until all are assembled. (The potstickers can be frozen at this stage on a sheet pan, and then transferred to a resealable plastic bag once frozen. To cook, follow the instructions below and add a 2 or 3 minutes of steaming time.)

To cook, set a large sauté pan over medium high heat and add the vegetable

oil. When the oil is hot, place the pot stickers in the pan, being sure to not crowd the pan. (If necessary, cook in batches.) Let cook until golden brown on the bottom, about 2 minutes, and then pour ¼ cup of water into the pan and cover with a lid. Let the pot stickers steam until the water has evaporated and they are warmed throughout. Repeat the process for any additional batches.

Serve with a homemade or store bought dumpling sauce for dipping.

DYP™ *and* Chipotle Casserole

~~~~~~~~~~~~~~~ *makes 6 to 8 servings* ~~~~~~~~~~~~~~~

1¼ cups Greek yogurt

2 cloves garlic, minced

2 teaspoons adobo sauce from a can of chipotles in adobo

Cooking spray

1½ pounds DYPs™, thinly sliced ⅛-inch thick on a mandoline

Salt and freshly ground black pepper to taste

1 cup shredded Swiss cheese

Preheat the oven to 350°F.

Whisk together the yogurt, garlic, and adobo sauce until smooth.

Coat the bottom and sides of an 8-inch square baking pan with cooking spray. Arrange the DYPs™ in an even layer on the bottom of the dish. Dollop 3 tablespoons of the yogurt mixture on top and season with salt and pepper. Repeat with the remaining DYPs™, yogurt mixture, and salt and pepper to form 5 layers. After the second layer, sprinkle on half of the cheese, and sprinkle the remaining half as the last layer. Press down on the layers to totally submerge the DYPs™ in the yogurt mixture. Cover with foil and bake for 30 minutes. Remove the foil and continue baking for 30 to 45 minutes, or until the yogurt has been absorbed, the DYPs™ are cooked through, and the top is browned.

Chicken Pot Pie

makes 4 to 6 servings

Filling:

2 tablespoons unsalted butter

1 medium onion, cut into ¼-inch dice

3 carrots, peeled and cut into ¼-inch dice

8 ounces DYPs™, cut into ¼-inch dice

8 ounces button mushrooms, quartered

1 celery stalk, cut into ¼-inch dice

1½ cups frozen petite peas

1 tablespoon finely chopped fresh tarragon

1 pound cooked chicken, cut into ¼-inch dice

Sea salt, ground white pepper, and nutmeg to taste

Sauce:

4 tablespoons unsalted butter

½ cup all-purpose flour

3 cups chicken broth

Crust:

2 sheets frozen pre-made puff pastry

Butter for brushing

1 egg, beaten

Preheat the oven to 400°F.

For the filling, in a heavy skillet over medium heat, melt the butter and add the onion, carrots, DYPs™, and mushrooms. Sauté for about 5 minutes, or until the onions are translucent. Add the celery and continue cooking for 3 more minutes. Add the peas, tarragon, and chicken and mix well. Season with salt, pepper, and nutmeg to taste. Set aside.

For the sauce, melt the butter in a heavy saucepan over medium-high heat. Stir in the flour and cook, stirring constantly, for 1 minute, or until you can no longer smell raw flour. Be careful not to let the flour scorch.

Add the broth, whisking constantly, until the sauce comes to a boil. Add the crème fraîche and season with salt and pepper.

Pour the sauce over the vegetable mixture and mix well. Divide the mixture into 6 to 8 individual ovenproof bowls.

For the crust, thaw the puff pastry sheets according to the package directions. Roll the puff pastry dough on a floured surface to ¼-inch thickness. Cut into circles ½-inch larger than tops of the ovenproof bowls. Butter the top edge of each bowl, and then brush it with the beaten egg. Place the pastry circles over the filling in each bowl, allowing the pastry to overlap the sides of the bowl. Crimp the edges, decorate with any remaining pastry, and place the bowls on a baking sheet.

Brush the top of each pastry with beaten egg and pierce with a fork or knife to allow the steam to escape. Bake for 30 to 45 minutes, or until the crust is browned. Serve in the bowls or turn each out onto a dinner plate.

Stuffed Pork Tenderloin

makes 4 to 6 servings

1 (12-ounce) pork tenderloin

8 ounces DYPs™, thinly sliced

½ Granny Smith apple, cored, halved, and thinly sliced

2 slices apple smoked bacon

1 fresh Portobello mushroom, stem and gills removed, sliced

Kosher salt and freshly ground black pepper to taste

2 tablespoons extra virgin olive oil

1 cup chicken broth

Sauce:

1 clove Melissa's Fresh Peeled Garlic, minced

2 tablespoons finely chopped fresh sage

Juice and zest of ½ lemon

½ cup white wine

1 cup heavy cream

3 tablespoons unsalted butter

Kosher salt and freshly ground black pepper to taste

Split the tenderloin in half lengthwise almost all the way through and open it up. Place the pork between 2 pieces of plastic wrap and, with a kitchen mallet, pound it to about ¼-inch thick. Place the DYPs™, apple, bacon, and mushrooms over the bottom third of the pork loin. Season with salt and pepper and roll up tightly, starting from the long side. Secure the pork with the butcher's twine and season the outside of the pork loin with more salt and pepper.

Preheat the oven to 325°F.

In an oven-safe skillet, heat the olive oil over high heat. Sear the pork loin on all sides and add the chicken broth. Place in the oven and bake for 20 to 30 minutes, or until the interior temperature reaches 155°F. Remove from the oven. Place the loin on a plate, tent with foil, and set aside.

While the loin is resting, make the sauce. Return the skillet to the burner over high heat. Add the garlic, sage, zest, juice, and wine; simmer until reduced by half. Add the cream and simmer until slightly thickened. Whisk in the butter and season with salt and pepper.

Slice the pork loin and place on a serving platter. Pour the sauce over the pork and serve.

Spiral DYP™ Pie

makes 6 to 8 servings

1½ pounds DYPs™

Salt and freshly ground black pepper to taste

1 cup shredded cheddar cheese

1 clove garlic, minced

2 tablespoons chopped chives

2 tablespoons chopped marjoram

⅓ cup heavy cream

2 eggs

2 sheets puff pastry

1 egg yolk

Preheat the oven to 425°F.

Place the DYPs™ in a large saucepan. Cover with cold water and bring to a boil. Reduce the heat and cook for 6 to 9 minutes, or until fork tender. Drain and slice ¼-inch thick.

Place half of the DYPs™, overlapping the slices, in the bottom of a pie dish, and season with salt and pepper. Sprinkle with half of the cheese, garlic, and herbs. Repeat the layers with the remaining DYPs™, cheese, garlic, and herbs.

In a separate bowl, whisk together the 2 eggs and cream, then pour the mixture over the DYPs™.

Cut each pastry sheet into quarters and each quarter into 3 equal lengths. Place the strips overlapping around the top of the pie in a spiral shape, leaving the center open. Press the edges down so that the pastry sticks to the pie dish, and then trim the edge. Whisk the egg yolk with 1 teaspoon of water and brush it on the top of the pie. Bake for 15 minutes. Reduce the oven temperature to 350°F and bake for 15 to 20 minutes more, or until the pastry is puffed and golden and the filling is set. If the sides of the puff pastry start to brown too quickly, cover them with a strip of foil. Allow the pie to stand for 15 minutes before serving.

Shepherd's Pie

makes 6 servings

5 cups DYPs™, peeled and halved

3 tablespoons unsalted butter or olive oil

½ to ¾ cup milk

4 cups cubed Portobello mushrooms

4 cups peeled and cubed butternut squash or sweet potatoes

2½ cups trimmed and chopped Brussels sprouts

2 cups peeled and chopped cipollini onions

Olive oil for drizzling

Kosher salt and freshly ground black pepper to taste

¾ cup vegetable or mushroom broth

1 tablespoon teriyaki sauce

1 tablespoon light soy sauce

1 tablespoon tomato paste

1½ tablespoons red wine (optional)

1½ tablespoons all-purpose flour

Pinch of fresh thyme leaves

Cooking spray

2 tablespoons minced fresh parsley

1 teaspoon smoked paprika

Preheat oven to 350°F.

Place the DYPs™ in a large saucepan. Cover with cold water and bring to a boil. Reduce the heat and cook for 10 to 12 minutes, or until the DYPs™ are fork tender. Drain the DYPs™ and return them to the saucepan. Add the butter or oil and milk and mash together. Season with salt and pepper and set aside.

On a parchment paper-lined baking sheet, place the mushrooms, squash or sweet potatoes, Brussels sprouts, and onions. Drizzle with olive oil, sprinkle with salt and pepper, and toss to coat. Bake for about 25 minutes, or until the vegetables are tender and caramelized. Remove from the oven.

In a small saucepan over medium heat, whisk together the broth, teriyaki sauce, soy sauce, tomato paste, and optional red wine and cook until heated through. Whisk in the flour to create a gravy. Stir in the thyme and turn off the heat.

Coat a baking dish with cooking spray. Add the roasted vegetables to the dish, and then cover with the gravy. Top it all with the mashed DYPs™, using a fork to create small peaks. Bake for 15 to 20 minutes, or until heated through, and then place the dish under the broiler for 1 to 2 minutes or until some of the peaks are golden brown. Remove from the oven and sprinkle with the parsley and smoked paprika. Let stand 5 to 7 minutes before serving.

DYP™ and Porcini Mushroom Pizza

makes 6 to 8 servings

1 package active dry yeast

1 teaspoon granulated sugar

1 cup warm water

2½ cups unbleached all-purpose flour

2 tablespoons olive oil

1 teaspoon sea salt

1½ tablespoons cornmeal

Olive oil for brushing

1 (½-ounce) package dried porcini mushrooms, rehydrated

8 ounces DYPs™, thinly sliced

¼ cup diced shallots

Extra virgin olive oil for drizzling

¼ cup chopped fresh Italian parsley

¼ cup chopped fresh oregano

Sea salt and freshly ground black pepper to taste

⅓ to ½ cup shaved Parmesan cheese

⅓ to ½ cup finely shredded mozzarella cheese

Melissa's Truffle Oil (optional)

Preheat the oven to 450°F.

Dissolve the yeast and sugar in the warm water, whisk together, and let stand for 8 to 10 minutes, or until foamy. Pour the yeast mixture into a large bowl. Stir in the flour, 1 teaspoon of sea salt, and 2 tablespoons of olive oil and let rest at least 5 minutes (but no more than 30 minutes).

Lightly flour a flat surface. Pat out the dough into a free-form shape about ¼-inch thick and about the length of a 12 x 17-inch baking sheet. Line a baking a baking sheet with parchment paper and sprinkle it with the cornmeal. Carefully place the stretched dough over the cornmeal. Brush the entire top with olive oil, crimping the edges as you go to form a crust.

Sprinkle half of the cheese over the crust, and then top with the DYPs™, mushrooms, and shallots. Top with the remaining cheese. Drizzle a little extra virgin olive oil over the top and sprinkle on the parsley, oregano, and salt and pepper to taste. Bake the pizza for about 25 minutes, or until the crust is golden, the DYPs™ are tender, and the cheese is melted. Remove from the oven and let rest about 5 minutes before slicing. Drizzle with truffle oil if desired.

Early Fall
Roasted Vegetables

~~~~~~~~~~~~~~~~~~~~ *makes 8 servings* ~~~~~~~~~~~~~~~~~~~~

¾ pound DYPs™,
cut in half lengthwise

1 Maui or sweet onion, cut crosswise into 3 equal pieces

1 acorn squash, cut lengthwise
into quarters, then into eighths,
seeds discarded

4 parsnips, cut in half lengthwise

2 tablespoons olive oil

1 tablespoon vegetable broth

½ teaspoon freshly ground
black pepper

½ teaspoon salt

1 tablespoon chopped fresh thyme

Thyme sprigs for garnish

Preheat the oven to 400°F. Place the DYPs™, onion, squash, and parsnips in
a large roasting pan and toss with the olive oil. In a small bowl, combine the
vegetable broth, black pepper, salt, and thyme. Toss the seasoning mixture
with the vegetables in the roasting pan.

Roast the vegetables for 35 to 40 minutes, stirring once, until the vegetables
are tender and nicely browned.

Remove the vegetables to a warmed large platter. Deglaze the roasting
pan with 2 tablespoons hot water, stirring to loosen the browned bits off the
bottom of the pan. Taste the liquid first to ensure that it does not have a burnt
taste. Pour the liquid from the pan over the vegetables and garnish with the
thyme sprigs.

Vegetable Tian

makes 4 to 6 servings

½ cup extra virgin olive oil, divided

3 cups sliced (⅛-inch-thick) eggplant (about 1 pound)

3 cups sliced (⅛-inch-thick) cipollini onions

3 cups sliced (⅛-inch-thick)DYPs™

3 cups sliced (⅛-inch-thick) Roma tomatoes

3 cups sliced (⅛-inch-thick) zucchini

3 tablespoons minced garlic

1½ tablespoons fresh thyme leaves

Coarse sea salt and freshly ground black pepper to taste

¾ cup panko breadcrumbs

1 cup Parmesan cheese, shredded

Preheat the oven to 375°F.

Brush 2 tablespoons of the olive oil on the insides of a low-sided round baking dish. Place one layer of eggplant slices vertically around the sides of the dish, then add a layer each of the onions, DYPs™, tomatoes, and zucchini toward the center. Repeat layers with remaining vegetables until the dish is completely filled to the center.

Sprinkle the minced garlic, thyme, and salt and pepper to taste over the vegetables, and then drizzle with 4 tablespoons of the olive oil. Cover the dish with foil and bake for 40 minutes.

Remove the foil. Sprinkle the breadcrumbs and cheese over the vegetables, and then drizzle the remaining 2 tablespoons of olive oil over the top. Continue baking another 20 to 25 minutes, or until the vegetables are completely tender, the cheese is melted, and the breadcrumbs are golden brown. Remove the tian from the oven and let rest at least 15 minutes before slicing and serving.

Just "Simply" Roasted DYPs™

makes 4 to 6 servings

1½ pounds DYPs™, cut in half

2 tablespoons extra virgin olive oil

Kosher salt and freshly ground black pepper to taste

Preheat the oven to 425°F.

In a bowl, toss all of the ingredients together. Place the DYPs™ in a single layer on a baking sheet. Roast for 10 to 13 minutes, or until fork tender and golden brown. Serve hot or at room temperature, anytime, all day long. They are the perfect snack!

Herbed Home-Fried DYPs™

makes 6 to 8 servings

2 pounds DYPs™

1 cup finely chopped onion

2 teaspoons chopped rosemary

Salt and freshly ground black pepper to taste

4 tablespoons olive oil, divided

¼ cup minced Italian parsley

Place the DYPs™ in a large saucepan. Cover with cold water and bring to a boil. Reduce the heat and cook for 8 to 12 minutes, or until fork tender. Drain and let cool. The DYPs™ may be prepared up to this point 1 day in advance and kept covered and chilled.

Cut the DYPs™ into quarters and toss with the onion, rosemary, and salt and pepper to taste.

In a large nonstick skillet, heat 2 tablespoons of the oil over moderately high heat until hot but not smoking. Sauté half the DYP™ mixture for 10 to 15 minutes, stirring occasionally, or until golden. Transfer to a covered serving dish to keep them warm.

Cook the remaining DYP™ mixture in the remaining 2 tablespoons of oil in the same manner. Transfer to the serving dish, and toss the parsley. Season with more salt and pepper to taste, if needed.

Italian Oven Fries

makes 4 servings

1½ pounds DYPs™, cut into ¼-inch-thick matchsticks

2 tablespoons vegetable oil

½ teaspoon salt

1 tablespoon Melissa's My Grinder® Organic Italian Seasoning

Cooking spray

1 cup freshly grated Parmesan cheese

1 tablespoon finely chopped parsley

Coarse salt and freshly ground black pepper to taste

Preheat the oven to 450°F. In a large bowl, toss the DYPs™ with the oil, ½ teaspoon salt, and Italian seasoning. Lightly coat a baking sheet with cooking spray. Spread the DYPs™ in a single layer on the sheet and bake 15 minutes or until golden and crisp. Remove the fries with a spatula. In a large bowl, toss the hot fries with the Parmesan and parsley. Season with salt and pepper to taste.

Candied DYP™
and Carrot Sauté

makes 4 to 6 servings

2 tablespoons extra virgin olive oil

2 tablespoons unsalted butter

3 carrots, trimmed and diced

1½ pounds DYPs™, diced

1 pinch kosher salt

2 tablespoons brown sugar

Add the oil and butter to a saucepan over medium heat. When the butter is melted, add the carrots, DYPs™, and salt and cook, stirring occasionally, about 10 minutes, or until the DYPs™ are tender. Stir in the brown sugar and sauté for 2 minutes longer, or until the brown sugar is dissolved. Serve hot.

Provençal DYPs™

~~~~~~~~~~~~ makes 4 to 6 servings ~~~~~~~~~~~~

2 pounds DYPs™

1 medium onion, sliced

6 cloves garlic, chopped

3 Roma tomatoes, cut into 1½-inch chunks

10 pitted olives, a mix of green and black (such as Kalamata and Niçoise)

½ teaspoon red chile flakes

¼ teaspoon garlic powder

1 tablespoon herbes de Provence

½ cup olive oil

2 teaspoons red wine vinegar

2 teaspoons kosher salt

Freshly ground black pepper to taste

1 tablespoon chopped fresh chives for garnish

Preheat the oven to 400°F.

Combine all ingredients except the chives in a large bowl and toss well. Spread the DYPs™ in an even layer in a roasting pan.

Roast, stirring once, for 30 to 35 minutes, or until the onions and tomatoes are somewhat caramelized and the DYPs™ are fork tender. Sprinkle with the chives.

DYPs™, Olives, Feta, *and* Mint

~~~~~~~~~~ *makes 4 servings* ~~~~~~~~~~

1½ pounds DYPs™, cut into quarters

4 sprigs mint, divided

8 ounces feta cheese, crumbled

¾ cup brine-cured black olives (such as Kalamata), pitted and chopped

¼ cup extra virgin olive oil

Salt and freshly ground black pepper to taste

Place the DYPs™ and 3 sprigs of mint in a large saucepan. Cover with cold, salted water and bring to boil. Reduce the heat and simmer for 6 to 9 minutes, or until fork tender. Drain the DYPs™ and discard the mint.

Chop the remaining sprig of mint. In a bowl, combine the chopped mint, feta cheese, olives, and oil. Stir the mixture into the warm DYPs™ and season with salt and pepper. Serve warm.

Smoky DYPs™

makes 8 to 10 servings

2 pounds DYPs™

1 large sweet potato, peeled and cut into 1-inch pieces

Salt to taste

1¼ cups warm buttermilk

4 tablespoons (¼ cup) melted butter

½ teaspoon black pepper, plus more for seasoning

1½ teaspoons minced chipotle pepper in adobo sauce

Place the DYPs™ and sweet potato in a large saucepan. Cover with lightly salted cold water and bring to a boil. Reduce the heat and cook for 8 to 12 minutes, or until fork tender.

Drain the potatoes and place in a large bowl. Using a potato masher, mash to the desired consistency. Stir in the warm buttermilk, melted butter, black pepper, and chipotle. Taste and adjust seasoning with salt and pepper if needed, stirring just until blended.

Baked DYPs™
with Blue Cheese

~~~~~~~~~~~~ *makes 12 to 15 appetizer servings* ~~~~~~~~~~

1½ pounds DYPs™

2 tablespoons olive oil

2 teaspoons coarse salt

½ cup Greek yogurt

1 to 2 ounces blue cheese

2 tablespoons chopped fresh chives

~~~~~~~~~~~~~~~~  ~~~~~~~~~~~~~~~~

Preheat the oven to 425°F.

In a medium bowl, toss the DYPs™ with the oil to coat evenly. Sprinkle the salt over the DYPs™ and toss well. Spread the DYPs™ out on a baking sheet and bake for 13 to 15 minutes, or until the DYPs™ are tender.

In a small bowl, combine the yogurt and blue cheese and mix well.

Cut a cross on the top of each DYP™. Press gently with your fingers to open the DYPs™.

Top each DYP™ with a dollop of the blue cheese mixture and garnish with the chopped chives.

Serve hot or at room temperature.

DYP™ Patties

~~~~~~~~~~~~~~~~~~~ *makes 12 patties* ~~~~~~~~~~~~~~~~~~~

1 pound DYPs™, quartered

½ teaspoon salt

¼ cup canola oil, divided

2 teaspoons paprika, divided

¼ chopped cup onion

½ cup shredded mozzarella cheese

~~~~~~

Place the DYPs™ and salt in a large saucepan. Cover with cold water and bring to a boil. Reduce the heat and cook for 3 to 6 minutes, or until tender. Drain the DYPs™ and then pass them through a potato ricer.

Heat 2 tablespoons of the oil in medium skillet over medium heat. Add the onion and 1 teaspoon of the paprika. Cook, stirring often, until the onions are tender and translucent. Stir the onions into the mashed DYPs™ and let cool. Once cool, stir in the cheese. Shape the mixture evenly into six 1-inch thick patties.

Heat the remaining 2 tablespoons of oil in a large nonstick griddle over medium heat. Add the patties and cook for 3 minutes, or until the bottoms are crisp and golden brown. Flip the patties over and cook for an additional 3 minutes, or until they are crisp and golden brown on both sides.

Note: *A common variety of potato ricer resembles a large garlic press. It has two long handles, one with a perforated basket at the end, the other with a flat surface that fits into the basket. The food is placed in the basket, and then the flat surface is pushed down into the basket by pressing the handles together, forcing the food through the holes.*

DYP™ Patties
with Bordelaise Sauce

~~~~~~~~~~~~~~ *makes 8 to 10 servings* ~~~~~~~~~~~~~~

DYP™ Patties:

1½ pounds DYPs™

2 tablespoons whole milk

2 fresh serrano chiles, minced

¼ sweet onion, diced small

2 egg yolks, beaten

3 tablespoons all-purpose flour

1 pinch kosher salt

Freshly ground black pepper to taste

2 cups panko breadcrumbs

1 tablespoon Melissa's Pico de Gallo Seasoning

1 large egg, beaten

Canola oil for frying

Bordelaise Sauce:

2 tablespoons extra virgin olive oil

5 tablespoons unsalted butter, divided

½ sweet onion, diced small

2 cloves garlic, minced

1½ cups fresh button mushrooms, quartered

2 cups beef broth

⅔ cup Bordeaux red wine

1 tablespoon A-1® Steak Sauce

Italian seasoning to taste

2 tablespoons cornstarch

4 tablespoons cold water

~~~~~~

Place the DYPs™ in a large saucepan. Cover with cold water and bring to a boil. Reduce the heat and cook for 8 to 12 minutes, or until fork tender. Drain and mash the DYPs™ with a potato masher.

To make the Bordelaise sauce, heat the olive oil and 2 tablespoons of the butter in a medium saucepan over medium heat. Add the onion and cook until caramelized, about 20 minutes. Add the remaining 3 tablespoons of butter, the garlic, and the mushrooms. Cook for 5 minutes, and then stir in the broth, wine, and A-1® Steak Sauce and bring to a simmer. Season with the Italian seasoning and cook, stirring occasionally, for about 30 minutes or until slightly thickened.

In a small bowl, dissolve the cornstarch in cold water. (The water must be cold because hot water will seize the mixture.) Stir the cornstarch slurry into the simmering sauce and cook, stirring frequently, until thickened.

Meanwhile, make the DYP™ patties. In a standing mixer, combine the mashed DYPs™, milk, chiles, onion, egg yolks, flour, salt, and pepper. Form the mixture into 2-inch diameter patties. In a separate bowl mix together the breadcrumbs and pico de gallo seasoning.

In a high-sided pan, add enough canola oil to come ½ inch up the sides and set over medium-high heat. Heat the oil to 375°F.

Dip the patties into the beaten whole egg and then coat with the breadcrumbs. Fry in small batches, flipping once, until the patties are golden brown on both sides, about 4 to 6 minutes. Drain on paper towels. Serve the DYP™ patties with the Bordelaise sauce.

Salty DYPs™ *with* Garlic Aïoli

~~~~~~~~~~~~~~ *makes 8 to 10 appetizer servings* ~~~~~~~~~~~~~~

3 quarts water

2 cups kosher salt

2 pounds DYPs™

1 cup mayonnaise

1 teaspoon fresh lemon juice

3 garlic cloves, minced

Salt and freshly ground
black pepper to taste

In a large saucepan, bring the water and salt to a boil, stirring occasionally to dissolve the salt.

Add the DYPs™ and bring back to a boil. Reduce the heat and cook for 8 to 12 minutes, or until fork tender. Drain and lay on paper towels to dry.

While the DYPs™ are cooking, make the aïoli by combining the mayonnaise, lemon juice, and garlic in a small bowl. Stir to combine and season with salt and pepper to taste. Serve the aïoli with the DYPs™.

Note: *Do not be afraid of the huge amount of salt used in this recipe. It doesn't permeate the flesh of the DYP™, and it gives the skin a nice seasoning and papery-crisp exterior. Use sea salt or kosher salt for best results.*

DYP™, Bacon, and Cheese Stuffed Mushrooms

makes 8 servings

8 ounces DYPs™, boiled

6 strips bacon, cooked and crumbled

1½ cups shredded sharp cheddar cheese

2 cloves garlic, minced

1 pinch kosher salt

1 pinch smoked paprika

24 large button mushrooms, stems removed

Preheat the oven to 350°F.

In a bowl, drain and mash the DYPs™. Mix in the bacon, cheese, garlic, salt, and paprika. Stuff the mushroom caps with the potato mixture.

Coat a baking sheet with cooking spray and place the stuffed mushrooms on the sheet. Bake for 20 to 25 minutes, or until the mushrooms are tender.

DUTCH YELLOW® POTATOES

WINTER

Corn Chowder

makes 4 to 6 servings

2 ounces thick-cut bacon
(about 3 slices), diced small

1 medium onion, diced small

3 cups corn kernels, divided

3 cups whole milk, divided

1 pound DYPs™, diced

2 teaspoons salt

½ teaspoon freshly ground
black pepper

½ cup heavy cream

Finely chopped chives
for garnish

Place the bacon in a large, heavy-bottomed saucepan or Dutch oven over medium heat. Cook, stirring occasionally, until the bacon is crispy, about 7 to 10 minutes. Remove with a slotted spoon to a paper towel-lined plate and set aside to drain. Remove all but 1 tablespoon of the bacon fat from saucepan.

Add the onion to the bacon fat in the saucepan and stir to combine. Cook, stirring occasionally, until the onions are softened, about 5 minutes.

Meanwhile, place 1 cup of the corn and 1 cup of the milk in a blender and blend until smooth.

Increase the heat to medium high and add the corn-milk purée, the remaining 2 cups of corn and 2 cups of milk, the DYPs™, and salt and pepper to the saucepan. Stir to combine and bring to a simmer. Reduce the heat to low and continue to simmer, stirring occasionally, until the DYPs™ are cooked through and the soup has thickened slightly, about 10 minutes. Add the cream, stir to combine, and return to a simmer. Taste and season with salt and pepper as needed. Serve garnished with chives and the reserved cooked bacon.

Jalapeño Cheese Soup

makes 4 to 6 servings

2 tablespoons olive oil

1 small onion, chopped

2 tomatoes, chopped

1 to 2 fresh jalapeños,
finely chopped

1½ pounds DYPs™

7 cups chicken or vegetable broth

2 tablespoons chicken-flavored
bouillon

1 cup shredded mozzarella cheese

Heat the oil in a medium stock pot over medium heat. Add the onion and
cook until translucent, about 5 minutes. Add the tomatoes and jalapeños and
continue to sauté for 3 more minutes. Add the DYPs™, broth, and bouillon and
bring to a boil. Reduce the heat, cover, and simmer until the DYPs™ are soft,
about 15 minutes. Remove from heat and add the cheese. Cover and let set
until the cheese melts, about 3 minutes.

DYP™ and Fennel Soup

~~~~~~~~~~~~~~~~~~~~~ makes 8 servings ~~~~~~~~~~~~~~~~~~~~~

3 tablespoons unsalted butter

2 fennel bulbs, trimmed and sliced

2 medium leeks, white parts only, washed well and sliced

2 cloves garlic, minced

1 pound DYPs™, diced

4 cups good-quality chicken stock

¾ cup evaporated milk

1 teaspoon fresh lemon juice

Salt to taste

White pepper to taste

Hot sauce or balsamic vinegar (optional)

Melt the butter in a large stock pot over medium heat. Add the fennel, leeks, and garlic and cook, stirring occasionally, until the vegetables are softened, about 15 minutes. Add the DYPs™ and stock. Cover and simmer until the DYPs™ are tender, about 40 minutes.

Remove the soup from the heat and allow to cool for about 20 minutes. Purée the soup in a food processor fitted with metal blade. (Be careful when puréeing hot liquids.)

Return the soup to the stock pot. Add the evaporated milk and lemon juice, and season with salt and pepper. For an extra touch of flavor, add a dash of hot sauce or balsamic vinegar.

Soupe au Pistou
(with Pesto and DYPs™)

makes 6 to 8 servings

Pistou:

6 cups fresh basil

2 cups fresh parsley

½ cup extra virgin olive oil

3 garlic cloves, peeled

Squeeze of lemon juice

Kosher salt and freshly ground black pepper to taste

Soup:

3 tablespoons olive oil

½ cup chopped leeks

½ cup chopped shallots

½ cup chopped baby carrots

Kosher salt and freshly ground black pepper to taste

2 cups peeled and cubed DYPs™

1 cup French green beans, cut into ½-inch pieces

½ teaspoon salt

2 cups peeled and chopped tomatoes

1 bay leaf

1 tablespoon fresh thyme leaves

2½ cups water

1½ cups cooked white beans

Place the pistou ingredients in a food processor and pulse to combine until completely smooth. Add more oil if necessary to reach a smooth consistency. Set aside.

Heat the olive oil in a large stock pot over medium heat. Add the leeks, shallots, and carrots and season with salt and pepper. Sauté until the vegetables are tender, about 4 to 5 minutes. Add the DYPs™ and green beans and stir to coat. Add the ½ teaspoon salt, tomatoes, bay leaf, thyme, and water and bring to a boil.

Adjust seasoning with salt and pepper, and then reduce the heat and simmer, covered, for about 20 minutes. Stir in the white beans, simmer for another 10 minutes, and adjust seasoning if necessary. Remove from the heat and discard the bay leaf. Spoon the soup into bowls and top each serving with a dollop of the pistou.

Winter Pot Roast

makes 4 to 6 servings

4 tablespoons olive oil, divided

2½ pounds boneless beef chuck

Salt and freshly ground black pepper to taste

3 tablespoons flour

1 large onion, sliced

1¼ cups red wine

2 cups beef stock

2 garlic cloves, minced

1 teaspoon salt

1 teaspoon dried thyme

1 teaspoon dried rosemary

1 bay leaf

1 pound DYPs™

8 ounces Melissa's Organic Peeled Baby Carrots

Heat 2 tablespoons of the olive oil in a large, heavy nonstick pot over medium-high heat. Season the beef with salt and pepper, and then dust with the flour. Add the beef to the pot and cook, turning, until brown on all sides, about 12 minutes. Transfer the beef to a plate.

Add the remaining 2 tablespoons of olive oil and the onions to the pot. Sauté over medium-high heat until the onions are slightly browned, about 5 minutes. Add the wine, beef stock, garlic, 1 teaspoon salt, thyme, rosemary, and bay leaf and bring to a boil. Return the beef to the pot and reduce the heat to medium-low. Cover partially and simmer gently for 1 hour. Add the carrots and DYPs™ and continue cooking an additional 1 to 2 hours, or until the meat is tender. Adjust seasoning with salt and pepper.

Beef Barbacoa

makes 6 to 8 servings

1 ounce Don Enrique Whole Dried Hatch Chiles, stems and seeds removed

Water to cover chiles

1 clove garlic

1 teaspoon dried oregano

2 tablespoons extra virgin olive oil

2 pounds beef stew meat, cut into 1-inch pieces

1 pound DYPs™, cut in half

1 fresh pasilla chile, diced

1 cup diced onion

2 tomatoes, diced

1 green bell pepper, diced

1 (12-ounce) beer

1 teaspoon freshly ground black pepper

½ teaspoon ground cumin

1½ tablespoons kosher salt

½ cup green olives

In a medium size pot, add the dried chiles and cover with water. Bring to a boil. Reduce the heat and simmer for 5 minutes. Next, place the chiles, 1 cup of the chile water, garlic, and dried oregano into a blender and mix until smooth.

Heat the olive oil in a large stock pot over medium heat. Add the beef and sear the meat on all sides. Add all of the remaining ingredients along with the blended chile sauce to the pot. Stir to combine and bring to a boil. Reduce the heat, cover, and simmer for 2 hours, or until the meat is very tender. Serve hot.

Picadillo

makes 8 to 10 servings

2 tablespoons canola oil

1 pound ground beef

1 pound ground pork

1 medium onion, chopped

2 Hatch Chiles, roasted, peeled, seeded, and chopped *(see page 95)*

2 cloves of garlic, minced

1 teaspoon salt

½ teaspoon freshly ground black pepper

2 teaspoons cumin

2 large tomatoes, peeled, cored and diced

1 pound DYPs™, diced

1 cup beef stock

Heat the oil in a large skillet over medium heat. Add the beef and pork and cook, stirring to break up the meat, until browned. Add the onion, chiles, garlic, salt, pepper, cumin, and tomatoes and cook for about 10 minutes, or until the onions are mostly clear. Add the DYPs™ and beef stock and bring to a boil. Reduce the heat and cook, stirring occasionally, for 10 to 15 minutes, or until the DYPs™ are tender.

Picadillo Empanadas

makes 30 empanadas

4 cups all-purpose flour

3 teaspoons kosher salt

2 tablespoons sugar

4 sticks (16 ounces) chilled
unsalted butter, cut into cubes

1 cup whole milk

1 recipe Picadillo
(see recipe page 211)

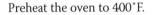

Preheat the oven to 400°F.

In a large bowl, combine the flour, salt, and sugar. Cut in the butter with a pastry blender or two knives until the mixture is crumbly. Add the milk and stir until the dough forms into a ball. Roll the dough out to about ⅛-inch thick and cut into 4-inch circles.

Place 3 tablespoons of the picadillo filling in the center of the each dough circle. Fold the dough over in half and pinch the edges to seal. Repeat with the remaining dough and filling.

Place the empanadas on baking sheet lined with parchment paper. Bake for 30 minutes, or until lightly browned.

Creamy Chipotle Chicken

makes 4 to 6 servings

4 pounds chicken thighs

1 sweet onion, peeled and halved, divided

3 cloves garlic, peeled and halved

1¼ cup sour cream

3 chipotle chiles in adobo

1 tablespoon olive oil

3 Roma tomatoes, chopped

1 pound DYPs™, diced

Kosher salt and freshly ground black pepper to taste

Steamed rice for serving

Place the chicken in a large stock pot and add enough water to cover. Cut one half of the onion into quarters and add to the pot. Add the garlic and bring to a boil. Reduce the heat and simmer for 20 minutes, or until the chicken is completely cooked. Remove the chicken and set aside, reserving the liquid.

In a blender, purée the sour cream, chipotle chiles, and 2 cups of the reserved liquid from the chicken. Slice the other half of the onion.

Heat the olive oil in a large skillet over medium heat. Add the sliced onion and cook until translucent, about 3 minutes. Add the tomatoes to the skillet and cook 2 more minutes. Add the DYPs™ and the sour cream mixture and bring to a boil. Stir in the chicken, reduce the heat, and simmer for 5 to 8 minutes, or until the DYPs™ are tender. Served over steamed rice.

Hearty Stew

makes 8 to 10 servings

½ cup all-purpose flour

2 teaspoons sea salt

¼ teaspoon freshly ground black pepper

4 pounds stewing beef or boneless, skinless chicken breast, cut into 1-inch cubes

3 tablespoons extra virgin olive oil

1 onion, quartered

2 carrots, roughly chopped

2 turnips, cubed

2 parsnips, roughly chopped

1 pound DYPs™, cut in half

1 (15-ounce) can stewed tomatoes

2½ cups beef or chicken broth

2 dried bay leaves

1 tablespoon cornstarch

¾ cup cold water

In a shallow dish, combine the flour, salt, and pepper.

Heat the oil in a large stock pot or Dutch oven over medium heat. Dredge the meat in the flour mixture, shaking off the excess flour, and place in the hot oil. Brown the meat on all sides. Next add the onion, carrots, turnips, parsnips, and DYPs™, and cook for 5 minutes, stirring often. Add the tomatoes, broth, and bay leaves and bring to a boil. Reduce the heat, cover, and simmer until the meat is tender, about 45 minutes to an hour.

In a small bowl, whisk together the cornstarch and water until smooth. Add some of the cornstarch slurry to the stew while stirring constantly. The stew should thicken. Only use enough of the cornstarch slurry to reach your desired consistency. Serve hot.

Asian-Style Chicken and DYP™ Sauté

~~~~~~~~~~~~~~~~ *makes about 4 to 6 servings* ~~~~~~~~~~~~~~~~

3 tablespoons extra virgin olive oil

½ sweet onion, sliced thin

4 boneless, skinless chicken thighs, chopped

1 red bell pepper, stemmed and seeded, sliced thin

1 green bell pepper, stemmed and seeded, sliced thin

1 yellow bell pepper, stemmed and seeded, sliced thin

1 Portobello mushroom, stem and gills removed, sliced thin

½ pound DYPs™, diced

¼ teaspoon freshly ground pepper

½ teaspoon granulated garlic

¼ cup soy sauce

1 tablespoon unsalted butter

Crushed red pepper flakes to taste

~~~~~~~~~~~~~~~ ~~~~~~~~~~~~~~~

Heat the olive oil in a large sauté pan over medium heat. Add the onion and sauté for 5 minutes, or until the onion is softened. Add the chicken and cook another 5 minutes. Add the bell peppers, mushroom, DYPs™, pepper, garlic, and soy sauce and sauté, stirring often for 10 minutes, or until the chicken is cooked through and the DYPs™ are tender. Stir in the butter and chile flakes and serve. This dish is great served over steamed rice.

PoTacos

makes 10 servings

⅓ cup olive oil

1 teaspoon hot sauce

1 tablespoon barbecue sauce

2 cups DYPs™, cut into
1½-inch sticks

2 cups Portobello mushrooms,
gills removed, sliced

1 cup diced white onion

1 cup seeded and diced
poblano pepper

1 cup seeded and sliced
red bell pepper

Kosher salt and freshly ground
black pepper to taste

3 tablespoons mayonnaise

1 tablespoon Greek yogurt

1½ cups shredded red cabbage

1 avocado, chopped

10 corn tortillas

Smoked paprika for garnish

Preheat the oven to 350°F.

In a small bowl, whisk the oil, hot sauce, and barbecue sauce together.
Place the DYPs™, mushrooms, onion, poblano, and bell pepper on a parchment
paper–lined baking sheet. Sprinkle with salt and pepper to taste, and then
drizzle the oil mixture over all. Toss well to coat the vegetables. Roast them
for about 20 minutes, or until the onions and peppers have softened and the
DYPs™ are tender and starting to brown. Remove the vegetables from
oven and keep warm.

In a medium bowl, combine the mayonnaise and yogurt. Add the cabbage
and avocado and toss to combine. Season with salt and pepper.

Lightly toast each tortilla directly over the largest burner of a gas stove
set on low heat. Let the tortilla cook for 10 to 15 seconds per side, flipping
back and forth several times until the tortilla is nicely warmed throughout
and charred in spots.

Divide the DYP™ mixture evenly and spoon on to the center of each
warm tortilla. Top each taco with the cabbage and avocado mixture.
Sprinkle with smoked paprika.

Thai-Like Veggie Stew

makes 6 to 8 servings

⅓ cup vegetable oil

1½ cups cubed yellow onion

2 cups peeled and cubed butternut squash

Kosher salt and freshly ground black pepper to taste

1½ tablespoons minced fresh ginger

1½ tablespoons minced fresh garlic

1 pound DYPs™, quartered

1 cup cubed red bell pepper

2 cups canned crushed tomatoes with their liquid

1 cup chopped green beans

2 cups coconut milk

½ cup peanut butter

1 tablespoon smoked paprika, or to taste (optional)

5 cups vegetable broth

1 package Melissa's Steamed Ready-to-Eat Black-Eyed Peas

2 cups baby spinach

Heat the oil in a heavy stock pot over medium heat. Add the onion and butternut squash, sprinkle with salt and pepper, and sauté for 5 minutes, or until the onion is softened. Add the ginger, garlic, DYPs™, and bell pepper and continue to cook for another 5 minutes. Add the crushed tomatoes and their liquid and the green beans, and bring to a low boil. Reduce the heat and simmer for 10 to 15 minutes, or until all the vegetables are tender.

Add the coconut milk and peanut butter and stir until well incorporated. Adjust the seasoning with more salt and pepper. If you'd like a little heat, add the optional smoked paprika. Add the vegetable broth, black-eyed peas, and spinach and stir to combine. Cook for 2 to 3 minutes, or until the peas are heated through and the greens are wilted. Serve over fluffy couscous or your favorite cooked grain.

Poblanos Stuffed *with* Goat Cheese Mashed DYPs™

makes 8 servings

8 medium poblano peppers

2 pounds DYPs™, quartered

2 teaspoons salt

1 cup buttermilk

2 tablespoons unsalted butter

3 Hatch Chiles, roasted, peeled, and chopped *(see page 95)*

4 ounces crumbled goat cheese, divided

Preheat the oven to 350°F. Preheat a grill to medium-high heat.

Grill the poblano peppers for 5 minutes on each side, or until they are charred. Place the peppers in a large zip-top plastic freezer bag and zip shut. Let stand for 10 minutes to loosen the skins. After 10 minutes, carefully peel the peppers. Cut each pepper lengthwise down one side, being careful not to cut through other side. Remove and discard the seeds and membranes.

Place the DYPs™ and salt in a large saucepan. Cover with cold water and bring to a boil. Reduce the heat and cook for 6 to 10 minutes, or until fork tender. Drain and return the DYPs™ to the saucepan. Mash with a potato masher, then stir in the buttermilk, butter, Hatch Chiles, and half of the goat cheese until blended. Spoon the mixture into a gallon-size zip-top plastic freezer bag and seal. Snip one corner of the bag and pipe the mixture into each roasted poblano pepper. Top each with the remaining goat cheese. Place the stuffed peppers in a baking dish and bake for 10 to 12 minutes, or until the cheese is melted.

Black-Eyed Pea Stew Cups

makes 12 servings

12 pre-made puff pastry cups

1 tablespoon extra virgin olive oil

½ medium sweet onion, diced small

1 clove garlic, minced

½ cup diced carrots

1 (14-ounce) can whole peeled tomatoes, undrained

¼ cup cooking sherry

1 cup diced DYPs™

1 (11-ounce) package Melissa's Steamed Ready-to-Eat Black-Eyed Peas

½ cup diced zucchini

½ cup diced yellow crookneck squash

Sea salt and freshly ground black pepper to taste

1 tablespoon ground cumin

4 tablespoons unsalted butter (optional)

Prepare and bake the puff pastry according to package instructions.

Heat the oil in a large stock pot over medium-high heat. Add the onion and cook, stirring often, about 20 minutes or until caramelized. Add the garlic and cook until aromatic, about 30 seconds. Next add the carrots and cook, stirring often, until tender and slightly caramelized.

Add the tomatoes to the pot, breaking them up with edge of a spoon. Add the sherry and bring to a boil. Reduce the heat and simmer until the mixture is reduced and thickened, about 15 minutes. Next add the DYPs™ and cook for about 5 minutes, or until the DYPs™ are tender. Add the black-eyed peas, zucchini, squash, salt, pepper, and cumin and cook until heated thoroughly. Add the butter, if desired, and stir until melted.

To serve, place a pastry cup on a small plate and fill with the stew.

DYP™-Turnip au Gratin

makes 6 servings

Unsalted butter for coating ramekins

2 turnips, peeled and very thinly sliced

1 pound DYPs™, thinly sliced

4 cloves garlic, minced

4½ cups shredded Gruyère cheese

Salt and freshly ground black pepper to taste

2 cups heavy cream

Preheat the oven to 350°F.

Butter the inside of six 4-ounce ramekins. Pour a little cream in the bottom of each ramekin. Fill the ramekins in this order: turnip slice, DYP™ slice, garlic, cheese, salt, pepper, and cream. Repeat this sequence until the dishes are full. Place the ramekins on a baking sheet and bake for 45 minutes, or until the vegetables are tender. Serve immediately.

Note: *For best results, slice the turnips and DYPs™ with a mandoline.*

Eric's DYP™
and Sausage Pizza

~~~~~~~~~~~~~~~ makes 1 (12-inch) pizza ~~~~~~~~~~~~~~~

1 fresh store-bought pizza dough

3 DYPs™, sliced ¹⁄₁₆-inch thick

1 tablespoon garlic oil

8 ounces fresh mozzarella,
roughly torn

1-2 links Italian sausage,
casings removed

1 egg (optional)

Preheat the oven to 450°F. Spread the dough out to about 12 inches on a pizza pan or a pizza peel (if using a pizza stone).

Brush the dough completely with garlic oil. Place the sliced DYPs™ evenly over the dough, leaving ½-inch border of crust. Top the DYPs™ with hand-torn mozzarella, and evenly distribute the raw sausage on top.

Bake for 10 to 12 minutes, or until the crust crispy and golden. If desired, crack the egg on top of the pizza during the final 4 to 5 minutes of cooking, and cook just until the white is set and yolk is runny.

Fresh Tomato
and Squash Tart

~~~~~~~~~ *makes 6 to 8 servings* ~~~~~~~~~

Butter for coating baking dish

1 large zucchini, cut in half lengthwise and thinly sliced

1 large summer yellow squash, cut in half lengthwise and thinly sliced

1 pound DYPs™, cut in half lengthwise and thinly sliced

¼ cup chopped onion

1 cup shredded Swiss cheese, divided

2 eggs, lightly beaten

1 teaspoon salt

½ teaspoon Italian seasoning

¼ teaspoon freshly ground black pepper

2 large fully ripened tomatoes, cut in half through stem ends and thinly sliced crosswise

Preheat the oven to 400°F. Butter a 9-inch pie plate or shallow casserole dish.

In a large bowl, combine the zucchini, summer squash, DYP™, onion, ¾ cup of the cheese, eggs, salt, Italian seasoning, and pepper until well mixed. Arrange half of the tomato slices on the bottom of the pie plate. Evenly spoon the vegetable mixture over the tomatoes, pressing them slightly to flatten. Arrange the remaining tomato slices on top, and then sprinkle with the remaining ¼ cup cheese. Bake for about 40 minutes, or until the vegetables are tender and glazed.

DYP™ and Tomato Gratin

makes 6 to 8 servings

2 tablespoons unsalted butter, melted

1½ pounds DYPs™, thinly sliced

1½ teaspoons chopped fresh basil

1½ teaspoons chopped fresh oregano

1 teaspoon salt

1 teaspoon black pepper

2 cups heavy cream

2 medium tomatoes, thinly sliced

½ cup breadcrumbs

1 cup shredded cheddar cheese

1 tablespoon chopped chives

Preheat the oven 350°F.

Brush the inside of a shallow baking dish or pie dish with the melted butter. Lay the DYPs™ in the dish, overlapping each other. Sprinkle with the basil, oregano, salt, and pepper. Pour the cream over all and cover with foil. Bake for 45 minutes. Remove the foil and arrange the tomatoes over the DYPs™. Sprinkle the breadcrumbs and cheese over the tomatoes. Return to the oven and bake, uncovered, for 15 minutes, or until the top turns golden brown. Garnish with chives and serve.

DYP™ and Hatch Chile au Gratin

~~~~~~~~~~ *makes 6 servings* ~~~~~~~~~~

Butter for coating pie dish

1½ pounds DYPs™,
very thinly sliced

2 ounces grated Gruyère cheese

2 cloves garlic, minced

1 cup heavy cream

6 Hatch Chiles, roasted, peeled,
seeded, and chopped *(see page 95)*

Salt to taste and freshly ground
black pepper to taste

Preheat the oven to 350°F.

Rub the butter along the bottom and sides of a pie dish. In a medium bowl, combine the cheese, garlic, and heavy cream.

Place a thin layer of DYPs™ and chiles in the prepared pie dish. Pour a little of the cream mixture over the vegetables. Repeat layers until all the DYPs™ and chiles are used, finishing with the remaining cream mixture on the top. Bake for 30 minutes, or until the DYPs™ are fork tender. Remove from the oven and let rest for 20 minutes before serving.

Spicy au Gratin

makes 6 to 8 servings

3 tablespoons unsalted butter

2 tablespoons all-purpose flour

3 cups whole milk

1½ tablespoons salt

Pinch of freshly ground
black pepper

1½ pounds DYPs™,
very thinly sliced

3 jalapeños, seeded and chopped

2 tablespoons chopped Maui or
sweet onions

16 ounces shredded cheddar
Jack cheese

Heat the butter and flour in a medium saucepan over medium heat, stirring
constantly, for about 2 minutes, or until the mixture loses its raw flour smell.
Be careful not to burn the flour. Add the milk and mix well. Simmer for
20 minutes, stirring often, until the sauce coats the back of a spoon. Stir in the
salt and pepper.

Preheat the oven to 350°F.

Pour a little of the sauce into the
bottom of a baking dish. Cover the
bottom of the dish with a layer of
DYPs™. Sprinkle with half of the
peppers and onions. Cover with one
third of the cheese, and then pour
over half of the remaining sauce.
Repeat the layering process, ending
with a layer of cheese. Cover and
bake for about 45 minutes.
Uncover and continue baking for
30 to 40 minutes longer, or until the DYPs™ are fork tender.

Auntie Marcie's DYP™ Latkes

~~~~~~~~~~ *makes 3 to 4 servings* ~~~~~~~~~~

1 pound DYPs™

1 small onion

¼ cup matzo meal

2 eggs, beaten

1½ teaspoon salt

¼ cup canola oil

Sour cream, for dipping

Applesauce, for dipping

Using a food processor with the grater attachment, shred the DYPs™ and onions. Combine with the matzo meal, eggs, and salt in a bowl, mixing well.

Heat the oil in frying pan until hot but not smoking. Drop quarter cup portions of the DYP™ mixture into the pan and flatten with a spatula. Fry over medium heat, flipping halfway through, until the DYPs™ are cooked and the latkes are browned on both sides. Drain on paper towels. Serve the latkes with a dollop each of sour cream and applesauce.

DYP™ Gnocchi

makes 4 servings

1 pound DYPs™

3 large egg yolks

½ cup freshly grated
Parmesan cheese

¼ teaspoon grated nutmeg

1 teaspoon chopped
fresh rosemary

½ teaspoon sea salt

¼ teaspoon freshly ground
black pepper

1 cup all purpose unbleached flour

1 tablespoon unsalted butter

Preheat the oven to 375°F.

Place the DYPs™ on a baking sheet and bake for about 12 to 15 minutes, or until well done. Allow them to cool, then cut in half and pass through a potato ricer. Make a mound of the mashed DYPs™ on the counter with a well in the middle. Add the egg yolks, Parmesan, nutmeg, rosemary, salt, and pepper to the center of the well. Using your hands, mix the DYPs™ into the center with the egg mixture. Sprinkle with the flour, little by little, folding and pressing the dough until it just holds together. If the mixture is too dry, add another egg yolk or a little water. Do not over mix.

Cut the dough into 4 equal pieces. Roll each piece into a rope about ½-inch in diameter. Cut each rope into ½-inch-long pieces and squish each one slightly with a fork. (You can also use a gnocchi board to shape the dough.) As you shape the gnocchi, dust them lightly with flour and scatter them on baking sheets lined with parchment paper.

When ready to cook, bring a large pot of water to a boil and add salt to taste. Drop in the gnocchi. When they rise to the surface, cook for about 90 seconds more. Remove the cooked gnocchi with a slotted spoon and drain.

In a saucepan, heat the butter over medium heat. Sauté the boiled gnocchi for a few minutes just until golden, and then serve.

DYP™ Curry

4 tablespoons canola oil

2 small onions, sliced

1 clove garlic, minced

2 pounds DYPs™, quartered

1 cup water

1 (14.5-ounce) can tomatoes, drained and liquid reserved

1½ tablespoons coconut milk

½ teaspoon turmeric

½ teaspoon ground cinnamon

½ teaspoon freshly ground black pepper

½ teaspoon cumin

½ teaspoon ground ginger

½ teaspoon sugar

½ teaspoon chile powder

½ teaspoon salt

In a large saucepan, heat the oil over medium-high heat. Add the onions and sauté until softened and transparent. Add the garlic and DYPs™ and sauté for 2 minutes more, or until the garlic is softened. Add the remaining ingredients and bring to a boil. Reduce the heat and simmer for 20 to 30 minutes, or until the DYPs™ are fork tender. If the curry is too thick, add some of the reserved tomato liquid to thin it out. The curry is delicious when served over rice.

Greek Artichokes and DYPs™, City-Style

makes 4 to 6 servings

3 tablespoons extra virgin olive oil

1 pound DYPs™, quartered

Kosher salt and freshly ground black pepper to taste

1 (8-ounce) jar marinated artichokes, drained and halved

Juice and zest of 1 lemon

10 Kalamata olives, pitted and chopped

3 tablespoons chopped flat-leaf parsley

1 tablespoon chopped fresh oregano leaves

½ cup crumbled feta cheese

Additional olive oil for drizzling

Heat the 3 tablespoons of oil in a large sauté pan over medium heat. Add the DYPs™ and sprinkle with salt and pepper. Sauté for 8 to 10 minutes, or until fork tender. Add the artichokes, lemon juice and zest, and olives, and cook for another 2 minutes, or until the artichokes are heated through. Stir the parsley and oregano into the mixture. Add the feta cheese, stir to combine, and remove from heat. Drizzle with the extra virgin olive oil and serve.

Hummus-Stuffed DYPs™

makes 24 to 26 appetizer servings

1¼ pounds DYPs™

1 (10-ounce) container hummus
(any flavor)

Smoked paprika or cayenne pepper
for garnish

Place the DYPs™ in a large saucepan. Cover with cold, salted water and bring to a boil. Reduce the heat and cook for 6 to 9 minutes, or until fork tender. Drain and let cool.

Cut the top third off of each DYP™ and just enough off of the bottom so that it can stand upright. Scoop out the insides without collapsing the sides. (Reserve the insides for another use.)

Fill a piping bag fitted with a fluted tip with hummus and pipe into each DYP™ cavity. Sprinkle with paprika or cayenne and serve.

Roasted Truffle DYPs™

~~~~~~~~~~~~~~~~~~~~~~~ *makes 4 servings* ~~~~~~~~~~~~~~~~~~~~~~~

1 pound DYPs™, cut in half

2 tablespoons extra virgin olive oil

¼ teaspoon sea salt

¼ teaspoon freshly ground black pepper

1 tablespoon Melissa's Truffle Oil

Preheat the oven to 425°F.

In a bowl, toss the DYPs™ with the olive oil, salt, and pepper. Transfer to a baking sheet and place in the oven. Bake until the DYPs™ are golden brown and fork tender, about 10 to 13 minutes. Toss with the truffle oil and serve.

Note: *You can also add slivers of fresh garlic to the DYPs™ prior to roasting or garnish them with shaved fresh black or white truffles.*

DYP™ Dinner or Sandwich Rolls

makes 24 dinner rolls or 12 sandwich rolls

1 package active dry yeast

¾ cup warm water, divided

½ cup cooked, mashed DYPs™, at room temperature

4 tablespoons unsalted butter, divided

¼ cup sugar

1½ teaspoons sea salt

1 egg, lightly beaten

3 cups unbleached, all-purpose flour, plus more for dusting

Cooking spray

2 tablespoons sesame seeds

In a small bowl, add the yeast to ¼ cup of the warm water. Set aside until mixture foams, at least 5 minutes.

Place the mashed DYPs™, sugar, salt, 2 tablespoons of softened butter, and ½ cup of the warm water in a large bowl and whisk to combine. Add the beaten egg and the yeast mixture, stir to combine, and then add the flour.

Stir the mixture together with a wooden spoon, then turn the dough out onto a lightly floured surface and knead by hand for about 5 to 6 minutes, or until the dough is smooth and easily stretches. Form the dough into a ball. Coat another bowl with cooking spray, place the dough in the bowl, and lightly spray the top of the dough. Cover with plastic wrap and let rest in a warm place for at least 1 hour, or until the dough has doubled in size.

Remove the dough from the bowl and place on a lightly floured surface. Divide the dough equally into 24 sections for small dinner rolls or 12 sections for sandwich rolls, and roll into balls.

Line two baking sheets with parchment paper and lightly coat them with the cooking spray. Place the rolls on the baking sheets—1 inch apart for the small rolls, 3 inches apart for the big rolls—and slightly flatten each with the palm of your hand. Brush the tops of the rolls with 2 tablespoons of the melted butter and sprinkle with sesame seeds. Cover the rolls with plastic wrap and return to a warm place for another hour, or until the rolls have doubled in size.

Preheat the oven to 375°F. Once heated, remove the plastic wrap and bake the rolls for 12 to 15 minutes, or until the rolls are light golden brown.

Roasted Root Vegetables *with* Herbs

makes 6 to 8 servings

12 ounces DYPs™, cut in half lengthwise

2 fennel bulbs, trimmed and cut lengthwise into wedges

1 yellow onion, sliced crosswise into 3 equal pieces

4 parsnips, cut in half lengthwise

3 large carrots, cut in half lengthwise

2 tablespoons olive oil

1 tablespoon vegetable broth

½ teaspoon freshly ground black pepper

½ teaspoon salt

2 teaspoons finely chopped fresh thyme leaves

Thyme sprigs for garnish

Preheat the oven to 400°F.

Place the DYPs™, fennel, onion, parsnips, and carrots in a large roasting pan. Toss the vegetables with the olive oil.

In a small bowl, combine the vegetable broth, pepper, salt, and chopped thyme. Toss with the vegetables in the roasting pan.

Roast the vegetables, stirring once, for 30 to 35 minutes, or until they are tender and nicely browned. Garnish with the thyme sprigs.

Papas Bravas

makes 6 to 8 servings

¼ cup olive oil, divided

1 tablespoon minced garlic

1 medium onion, julienned

1 red bell pepper, julienned

3 cups canned tomatoes in juice, chopped and juice reserved

½ cup chicken broth

5 chipotle peppers in adobo sauce, minced (adjust amount to desired spiciness)

3 pounds DYPs™, cut in half

1 tablespoon salt, plus more for seasoning

1 teaspoon freshly ground black pepper

Preheat oven to 425°F.

Heat 2 tablespoons of the olive oil in a large saucepan and add the garlic, onions, and bell pepper. Cook 5 to 6 minutes, or until the vegetables are tender. Add the tomatoes and their juice, chicken broth, and chipotle peppers. Season to taste with salt and simmer until the mixture is reduced and slightly thickened, about 10 minutes.

Meanwhile, in a roasting pan, toss the DYPs™ with the remaining 2 tablespoons olive oil, 1 tablespoon salt, and pepper. Roast for about 15 to 20 minutes, or until the DYPs™ are fork tender. Transfer to the tomato mixture and fold together gently. Adjust the seasoning with salt and pepper if necessary.

Papas Mexicanos

makes 6 servings

2 pounds DYPs™, cut in half

2 tablespoons extra virgin olive oil

Salt and freshly ground black pepper to taste

1 (12-ounce) package Melissa's Soyrizo

Preheat the oven to 425°F.

In a large bowl, toss the DYPs™ with the olive oil, salt, and pepper. Place on a baking sheet and roast for about 12 to 17 minutes, or until fork tender.

Prepare the soyrizo according to the package directions. As the soyrizo begins to break up, add the DYPs™ to the pan. Cook together until heated through. Serve hot.

Party Roasted Veggies

makes 16 servings

3 tablespoons chopped parsley

3 tablespoons chopped thyme

3 tablespoons chopped basil

¼ cup balsamic vinegar

1 garlic clove, minced

½ cup olive oil

16 baby zucchini, trimmed and cut in half lengthwise

16 baby yellow squash, trimmed and cut in half crosswise

1 package Melissa's Peeled and Steamed Red Beets, quartered

1 yellow bell pepper, cut in 1-inch pieces

8 cipollini onions, peeled and cut in half crosswise

2 turnips, trimmed and cut into bite size pieces

1 pound DYPs™, cut in half

3 carrots, trimmed and cut into bite size pieces

1 bunch pencil-thin asparagus spears, trimmed

Salt and freshly ground black pepper to taste

Preheat oven to 425°F.

Whisk together the parsley, thyme, basil, vinegar, garlic, and olive oil in small bowl.

Place all the vegetables on a baking sheet in a single layer. Drizzle the olive oil mixture over the vegetables and season with salt and pepper. Roast for 15 minutes, or until the vegetables are browned and fork tender. Serve warm or at room temperature.

Horseradish Mash

makes 6 to 8 servings

2 pounds DYPs™

4 ounces fresh horseradish root, peeled and cut into 3-inch pieces

½ teaspoon salt

¾ cup half-and-half

4 tablespoons unsalted butter

Salt and freshly ground black pepper to taste

Place the DYPs™ and horseradish in a large saucepan. Cover with cold, salted water and bring to a boil. Reduce the heat and cook for 8 to 12 minutes, or until fork tender; drain. Run the DYPs™ and horseradish through a food mill or potato ricer (or mash by hand) back into the saucepan.

In a small saucepan, heat the half-and-half and butter over medium-high heat just until the butter melts and the half-and-half is hot. Do not boil. Remove the mixture from the heat and pour over the DYPs™ and horseradish. Season with salt and pepper to taste and stir over low heat just until warm. Serve immediately.

DYP™ and Cardoon Mash

~~~~~~~~~~~~~~~~~~~ *makes 6 servings* ~~~~~~~~~~~~~~~~~~~

¼ pound cardoon

2 tablespoons white vinegar

1½ pounds DYPs™, cut in half

Salt to taste

¼ cup whipping cream

2 tablespoons unsalted butter

Celery salt to taste

Freshly ground black pepper to taste

6 Melissa's Pimientos Del Piquillo, diced

To prepare the cardoon, first trim off the bottom, and then peel the stringy fibers off the stalks with a vegetable peeler. Cut the stalks into 1-inch pieces, and then soak them in a bowl of water with the vinegar for thirty minutes. The vinegar helps to reduce the bitter taste of the cardoon and prevents discoloration.

Drain the cardoon and place the in a large saucepan. Cover with lightly salted water and bring to a boil. Reduce the heat and simmer for 15 minutes. Add the DYPs™ and cook for 5 to 8 minutes more, or until fork tender. Drain the vegetables, reserving ¼ cup of the liquid. Return the vegetables to the saucepan.

Add the cream and butter and mash the vegetables until almost smooth. Season with celery salt and pepper to taste. Stir in the piquillo peppers and mix until well combined. Over medium heat, continue cooking the DYP™ mixture until heated through, adding the reserved cooking liquid if the mixture is dry.

DYP™ Ponuts (aka...Doughnuts)

makes 4 dozen doughnuts

1 cup cooked, mashed DYPs™

1 cup milk

2 eggs, beaten

1 tablespoon plus 2 teaspoons baking powder

½ cup light brown sugar

½ cup granulated sugar

½ teaspoon coarse sea salt

3 tablespoons melted butter

2½ teaspoons vanilla extract

4 cups unbleached all-purpose flour

1 cup powdered sugar

½ cup unsweetened cocoa

⅓ cup ground cinnamon

Flour for coating hands

Vegetable oil for frying

Combine the DYPs™, milk, and beaten eggs in a bowl. Add the baking powder and stir to combine until foamy. Add the brown sugar and granulated sugar and stir to combine thoroughly. Stir in the salt, melted butter, and vanilla extract. Fold in the flour, 1 cup at a time, until the dough is a bit sticky but manageable.

In a separate shallow bowl, whisk together the powdered sugar, cocoa, and cinnamon until thoroughly mixed.

Have a baking sheet lined with paper towels ready for draining the fried doughnuts. Have a second baking sheet lined with parchment paper ready to hold the doughnuts after they've been coated.

Coat your hands with flour and grab enough of the dough (about 1 or 2 tablespoons) to form golf ball–sized balls. Heat at least 4 inches of the oil in a deep pot, on medium high heat until the oil sizzles when a bit of dough is dropped in the pot. Raise the heat slightly for frying.

Drop dough balls into the hot oil, and repeat with about 8 dough balls or as many as fit without crowding the pot. Use a wooden spoon to make sure the balls are not sticking to the bottom of pot. Continue frying for about 3 to 4 minutes per side, or until the balls are golden brown. Remove each ponut to the paper towels for about 20 seconds, and then dredge each one in the cinnamon mixture. Repeat with the remaining dough, a batch at a time, until all the ponuts are fried and coated.

Chocolate DYP™ Cake

makes 12 servings

2 sticks (16 tablespoons) butter

2 cups sugar

4 eggs, beaten

3 ounces unsweetened chocolate, melted

1 cup cold cooked and mashed DYPs™

1 teaspoon ground cinnamon

¼ teaspoon nutmeg

2 cups sifted all-purpose flour

1 teaspoon baking soda

1 cup buttermilk

1 cup chopped hazelnuts (optional)

Preheat the oven to 350°F.

In the bowl of an electric mixer cream the butter. Gradually add the sugar and beat until light and fluffy. Add the eggs and beat until well combined. Add the chocolate, DYPs™, cinnamon, and nutmeg, and mix to combine.

In a separate bowl sift the flour and baking soda together. With the mixer running at a low speed, add a little of the flour mixture, then a little of the buttermilk, alternating between the mixtures until well combined. Add the hazelnuts, if using, and mix lightly. Pour into a 9-inch buttered springform pan. Bake for 1 hour, or until a cake tester comes out clean. Let cool completely in the pan before removing the cake.

Gluten-Free Peanut Butter Cookie Sandwiches

makes 10 to 12 cookie sandwiches

2 cups rolled oats, divided

½ cup packed brown sugar

6 DYPs™, boiled and pressed through a ricer

1 cup peanut butter

1 cup raisins

Filling:

2 sticks (8 ounces) butter, softened

3½ cups powdered sugar

1 pinch kosher salt

1 teaspoon pure vanilla extract

1 teaspoon whole milk

Preheat the oven to 350°F.

Process ¾ cup of the oatmeal in a spice grinder. In the bowl of a standing mixer, add the ground oatmeal, the remaining rolled oats, brown sugar, DYPs™, peanut butter, and raisins. Mix until well combined. Form the dough into 20 to 24 balls. Place them 2 inches apart on a baking sheet lined with parchment paper. Flatten the balls a bit using the back of a fork. Bake for about 8 minutes, or until the bottom of the cookies are golden brown. Cool completely on wire racks. (Because there is no flour in this recipe, the cookies are very delicate, especially when they are warm.)

To make the filling, beat the butter, powdered sugar, and salt with an electric mixer until well combined. Add the vanilla and milk and beat until creamy.

Place one cooled cookie, upside down, on a cutting board. Place a heaping tablespoon of the filling in the center of the cookie and top with another cookie (right side up). Carefully, gently press it down. Repeat with the remaining cookies and filling.

DYP™ Coconut Fudge

makes 32 (1-inch) pieces

½ cup hot cooked and mashed DYPs™, unseasoned

3 cups powdered sugar

1 cup flaked or shredded coconut

1 teaspoon pure vanilla extract

2 ounces semisweet chocolate

Lightly butter a 4 x 8-inch loaf pan. While the DYPs™ are hot, beat in the sugar and coconut, and then stir in the vanilla. Press into the buttered loaf pan.

Melt the chocolate in the microwave and pour over the top of the DYP™ mixture. Chill completely, and then cut into squares. Store in an airtight container in the refrigerator.

Index